Pathway to a Legacy of Dignity

An Open Letter to African Americans

Anthony Blackburn

WESTBOW·
PRESS
A DIVISION OF THOMAS NELSON
& ZONDERVAN

WestBow Press books may be ordered through booksellers or by contacting:

WestBow Press
A Division of Thomas Nelson & Zondervan
1663 Liberty Drive
Bloomington, IN 47403
www.westbowpress.com
1 (866) 928-1240

ISBN: 978-1-4908-4479-4 (sc)
ISBN: 978-1-4908-4480-0 (hc)
ISBN: 978-1-4908-4481-7 (e)

Library of Congress Control Number: 2014912796

Printed in the United States of America.

WestBow Press rev. date: 08/20/2014

Contents

Introduction

I owe it to prospective readers to take a bit of time here at the beginning to speak about my use of the word *legacy*, which appears in the title. When one decides to write a book of nonfiction, it is important for the author to let his or her readers know that he or she is committed to the dedication it takes to give factual information. Of course, that factual material becomes a basic part of the ideas the author wants to convey and the reason for originally taking on the task of writing the book in the first place.

You should know that this book was not born from some kind of sudden inspiration that came overnight. It was born from some gnawing thoughts I had over a period of time— thoughts that recurred almost daily.

I could not escape these feelings as I read newspapers daily and watched the news on television. More and more, I kept reading and seeing thoughts regarding where the black race was heading in America at this point in time. I noticed many negatives in New York City with our people. These people were, of course, other African Americans. I began to see a pattern - most of them were just as upset as I was over this negative and counter-productive behavior. There are too many clear-cut issues that are getting worse, not better, among black people as a group.

I then began to ask African Americans questions about different issues, telling them to answer on a scale from one to ten, with one being the worst and ten being the best. Since I had already seriously thought about each issue, I was not surprised when I never got any answer over a three. I invite you to look at the titles in the table of contents to see what kinds of categories and issues I discussed. Once you move on into the text, chapter by chapter, you will see that I give all of the issues and problems detailed treatment.

My decision to stop discussing and start writing came about when I received the delivery of my newspaper on July 2, 2012. On the weekend prior to the Independence Day holiday, I read things that shocked me out of boredom. On Saturday and Sunday of that weekend, there had been multiple shootings involving black people shooting other black people in each and every borough of New York City, with the one exception being Staten Island. If I asked you to guess what ethnicity makes up most of the residents of Staten Island, I am sure you could correctly guess that that borough is mostly Caucasian. The other boroughs where the carnage took place were Brooklyn (Kings County), Manhattan (New York County), the Bronx, and Queens. Since July 2, 2012, this news has haunted me. Every day, I read about more blacks who were shot and killed. Many of them were children who had just started to live. Many of them never had a chance to even go to school. I could not begin to fathom where our so-called black leaders were. This was some of the worst black-on-black terror I had seen in my fifty-three years of living in New York. And all the black leadership could do was knock the New York Police Department for their efforts at keeping more black people from getting shot by what became known as "stop and frisk." The NYPD was attempting to be proactive rather than reactive when they heard another person had been killed. But our black leaders in New York, and also at the NAACP, just wanted to stress constitutional rights. Please be sure to read chapter 7. Everybody knew that black gang members were randomly shooting any blacks in their line of fire. The leaders of black street gangs, who were co-opting people into their Bloods or Crips organizations, made sure everyone knew this information. These were young men who were already sitting ducks in the New York City housing projects. The gang leaders had already been working on them for years. They knew that when a guy turned fifteen or sixteen years old, they could get him to drop out of school and join their gang.

Those of you who will take the time to read this book already know that as an ethnicity in America in the twenty-first century, we are not doing enough to ensure any kind of legacy of dignity. We are killing each other, we are dropping out of school, and too many of us revere prison more than we revere school. Especially when it comes to going on to college. We have some of the poorest women and children in America because we have women who refuse to be discerning when deciding to have children with men whom they should know do not care about them or how they will survive. How is a man who dropped out of school in the ninth or tenth grade going to take care of a woman and her child or children?

Some have become experts at finding a bunch of flimsy, illusory excuses to blame for all of our poor social behavior, for our criminal behavior, and also for whatever we are not achieving. At the top of the excuse list is racism. Does racism exist? Of course it does. But when someone today claims, "I can't succeed, because the Man always has his foot on my neck," we have to ask the following question: How did others manage to succeed with the Man's foot on their necks? All black people should know by now that racism exists in this country, and it always will. The country was founded on racism. If that were not true, how could we have ever been slaves? If that were not true, how could this American ruling class still be so casual, even today, over how they came in and took this country from the Native Americans? That's all true, but it just happens to be another book. I wrote this book in the hope of focusing on how we have been continuously shooting ourselves in the foot.

Following closely behind our rants on racism are laments on our poverty: "We are poor people who are forever trapped in the ghetto." The next question, then, is this: Who specifically has you, or us, trapped in the ghetto? Why not take time to seriously ponder what you have done and what you have not done that you could have done? That just might be the answer to that question. At some point, we have to admit that racism still exists, but slavery does not still exist. So many of our ancestors have worked so hard, and they persevered for so long, to help us shed those chains from our wrists, legs and minds.

I hope that by now, you see that I am fully committed to saying what is true in these chapters that will follow. If what one says is true, there is no reason for guilt. With that in mind, I ask you to take a serious look at the people you have accepted as self-appointed black leaders. What are you reasonably expecting of a real black leader? What success or value has your black leader given to you as an individual? I know that so-called black leaders spend a lot of time presenting you with the next best excuse you can use, especially if they can spin it in any way as something that has to do with racism. You are ripe to buy into the excuse, and you go to bed on that night only to awaken the next day in the same condition you were in the day before. This black leader you rely on so much only keeps you from ever using your own mind and thinking for yourself. He keeps giving you the same spiels, and you get deeper and deeper into some kind of brainwashed rut where you don't even feel you can do anything beneficial for yourself. When you get to that point, you are just another part of his or her (mostly his) brainwashed base. He can count on you whenever he wants to do a protest. But again, what can he do to help you become more successful as an individual?

Lastly, I had some discussions, as a prelude to writing this book, with a few who made remarks like, "These kinds of issues have been going on forever." Others asked me, "What is it you hope to accomplish?" And others said, "What is it you hope to change?' My answer to all of them is that I might not change anything, but I will have the satisfaction of letting our people know that I cared. Then I can proudly say, "I gave it my best shot." Please read on.

To acquire the habits of reading is to construct
for yourself a refuge from almost all the miseries
of life.

—W. Somerset Maugham

Learning Begins at Birth

Each one of us needs to know and accept that life is a
sequential thing. To try to deny this fact is to start off on
the wrong foot. We must recognize that life always contains
a beginning, middle, and end. This chapter is number one
because this is where this book begins. It is an open letter to
black parents.

Many books have information about a child's early
developmental years, meaning information that applies to
the child from infancy to the age four or five. I would like to
emphasize and focus on what I call the "formative days." I have
asked people, "Do you remember how old you were when you
spoke your first word?" The answer from all of them has been
no. Next, I asked if they had any idea what their first word was.
The answer, again, was always no.

Looking within the African American community, I chose
people at random. I did not select subjects by appearance or any
other characteristic. I chose people randomly in order to prove
that we all begin to learn long before we know we are learning.
Our children are just like us in this respect. They have the
capacity to learn from the time they are born. I want to make
this point because I want black mothers and fathers to know
that their children can be as smart as the children of any other

1

ethnic group. They need to invest the time and effort to develop their children into those smart people they can be.

Each of us enters the world with a tabula rasa—a blank tablet, or clean slate. There exists a connection to the brain or mind, and there can be no impressions before birth, because a baby must record impressions upon that blank tablet from life's experiences before the mind begins to learn and remember.

Every child born begins to record things after coming in contact with other human beings. This is the point when parents or other significant people become important. The parent, parents, or other people surrounding the child are responsible for the first impressions and life experiences that get imprinted upon the tabula rasa. Once the child begins to hear and listen to the parents, he or she no longer has a tabula rasa. After all, that is when the newborn infant gets the ability to gain new experiences through the five senses of seeing, hearing, smelling, tasting, and feeling. Other than this, at the beginning, the newborn spends most of her or his time sleeping. Expressions of hunger or some kind of discomfort fill most of a baby's waking hours.[1]

As the infant moves on to the age of one, he or she usually will master how to crawl and then learn how to walk. This is normally the case, unless the child was born with some kind of physical disability that makes moving on his or her own more difficult.

By the end of the second year, a child has already mastered the most elementary steps of early childhood. Children then put together a few words and speak to people in sentences that become more and more intelligible. At the same time, they begin more and more to understand what others are saying to them. This is an important time, as a parent comes to realize the possibility of beginning to make a real impact on a child's development. We can tell that from day to day, a child grows

---

[1] *World Scope Encyclopedia*, Unabridged Deluxe Edition (New York: WorldScope Corp., 1961).

rapidly. We can also tell at this stage if more repetitive work needs to be done, if the child is a fast learner, and if she or he is accepting of others. It is important, black parents, for your child, by the age of two, to have a sense of character, morality, and manners—a sense of what is right and what is not right. It is important that you do not raise a child in a house built on shifting sand.

You should give your child all of the attention he or she requires so that he or she will be able to survive and thrive in this world. We should also try to prepare our children to survive at a high rate of success as they grow older. Unfortunately, African American parents, there are many polls showing that you have a lot of work to do. Even without the polls, we can see that our young black people are nowhere near the top or middle when it comes to a legacy of dignity, respect, pride, and prosperity.

We need to look more toward preparing our children for the real world. We need to prepare them for this future much earlier than we currently do. You decided that these were children you wanted in your families. So if this is the case, you should spend time and energy helping them be proud of themselves as they grow up, rather than raising them to feel they are wasted beings.

Returning to an earlier point, let me add that there is more to parenthood than just deciding, "I need to have a baby," and then, after the baby is born, choosing to let the television or vulgar rap CDs raise your child. At that point, you have decided to take no part in your child's life as a dedicated and responsible parent. At this point in our history, too many African American parents are saying to their children, "I gave birth to you, but now it is up to you to raise yourself." What a pity!

Every child brought into this world should have the expectation that he or she will have an adequate parent. Though a child begins life with a tabula rasa, or clean slate, he or she soon observes, "This is my mother," or "This is my father," or whoever. "Aren't I supposed to be learning from this adult what to do in life?"

This might sound harsh, but take some time to think about it: if you know that you are not willing to spend time to ensure your child's success in this world, or if you do not have those skills, you should not bring that black child into this world. Parents of black children, you need to stop being so deficient in raising your children. You cannot blame everything on poverty and racism. I will cover more on that issue in later chapters.

As I write this, I am wondering what, from house to house, home to home, we are telling our young children to prepare them for the day when they will go off to school. I hope parents have many preparatory discussions before their children reach the age of five. I have a feeling, however, that in many black homes, there has been little preparation. I hope I am wrong. But given the way many of our youngsters enter school, especially the young boys, it seems they are totally unprepared to enter an environment dedicated to learning. Because of this, they not only are unprepared but also do not know that they have entered a place where they are expected to show self-discipline and respect for other pupils.

The W. Somerset Maugham quotation at the beginning of this chapter highlights a truth important in all of our lives. Reading is one of the most important—if not the most important—things that all of us can master. Reading is the art that any of us can master and then practice for the rest of our lives.

I am sure that anyone reading this book already knows about the importance of mastering the three Rs: reading, 'riting, and 'rithmetic. No child or adult can ever hope to be really intelligent or successful without mastering these three elementary disciplines. Again, the best time to introduce children to the three Rs is when other nonsense has not yet cluttered their minds.

—∿∿∿—

What needs to be in the spotlight around the age of two is the parent's need to prepare the child for school. Young children have no idea what school is or what going to school will mean in their lives if the parents do not get them ready for that important phase of their lives. Frankly, too many black parents do not do enough to prepare their children for school. As a result, the children are not ready to enter school. Such children then ask in their young minds, *School? What is school?*

This is the time when these youngsters are ready to learn. Their learning progresses rapidly when they are this age. This is the best time to introduce them to books. It is the best time to get them interested in reading. It is also the best time for us to sit down with them and introduce them to the best learning programs on television. It is not time to just sit them in front of the television and let it babysit for you.

This is also the best time to introduce them to the library. You should take time to introduce them to this key institution. You should take them to the library with you, let them get to know what a library is, and help them discover what they can find in a library. Let them get used to knowing that there are whole sections in libraries that are devoted to children. And since it is free, check out some books that will be helpful for the child's early childhood development.

It is unfortunate that many African American parents are failing to make sure they make earnest efforts to give their children a strong foundation to stand on and to live by. This kind of foundation is necessary if they are going to be successful in life. For instance, we cannot continue to destroy our children's hopes by letting them hear us say that they are not receiving what other ethnicities are getting. I am not saying that this is not true in any case, but we should not destroy our children's hopes at an early age.

I would be one of the last to deny the fact that racism still abounds in America. Racism is part of America's DNA. I know that it can derail a black person's chances for getting a better position or even getting hired. Poverty does many things to ruin dreams. However, one needs to look in the mirror and ask himself or herself, "What is the real reason I am in poverty?" Then keep looking in the mirror, and give yourself an honest answer. Education, learning, and proficiency in different skills could lift many out of poverty who are currently at that level.

Think honestly about what I just stated above. We need to stop being a joke for the other ethnicities in this country. We need to stop supplying the jokes that make us a laughingstock. In short, poverty, racism, and unfairness will always be around, but as we accept that fact, we also need to accept the fact that more African Americans should be doing more positive things.

Chapter 1 Inspirational Choice

Booker Taliaferro Washington's Achievements

In the introduction, I promised you I would include some information on an earlier inspirational African American. I felt that I could not find a better, more exemplary person than Booker T. Washington to show what young black people today should see as an extraordinary hero when it comes to the importance of learning and getting an education.

It is important to note that Booker T. Washington was born as a slave in 1856. The Civil War did not begin until 1861. The Civil War did not end until 1865. That means that Booker was in slavery for nine years. We should not feel that on the day slavery ended in 1865, everything was peaches and cream. For most slaves, the problems had just begun. They were free for the first time—but what did freedom mean? They could leave their owners' plantations for the first time—but where were they supposed to go, and what were they supposed to do? What did they own? The answer is "nothing." Just imagine some black people going down the road to nowhere and nothing. It had to be an awful feeling to realize that in being free, they might be just as bad off as they were as plantation slaves. They had never owned anything, and now they were free with nothing.

That was where Booker, this young boy of nine years old, and his mother found themselves. Born in these circumstances, Booker T. Washington could have said to himself, "I'm doomed. What is there for me to look forward to as any kind of good future?" But Booker T. Washington was better and stronger than that.

Booker was born in a small town called Hales Ford, Virginia. His mother's name was Jane Ferguson, and his father was an unknown white man. Back in those woeful times, white men had their way with the black slave women. A man named James Burroughs owned the plantation that Booker grew up on.

Even as a young boy, during his time as a slave, he was beaten, likely because he was not doing his work properly or quickly enough. But Booker became interested in education when he had his first exposure to a schoolhouse near his plantation of birth. While peeking through a window, he was able to observe children sitting at desks and reading books. This sight was like a branding iron on his young mind. He swore to himself that one day, he would be doing what these children were doing. At the time, it was illegal to teach slaves to read and write.

After the end of the Civil War, Booker, his mother, and the rest of her poor family moved to Malden, West Virginia. Booker was just nine years old. In Malden, West Virginia, his mother married Washington Ferguson. It might be helpful to state here that Jane, his mother, was probably one of the slaves in the line of ancestors of George Washington, the first US president. She only became Jane Ferguson after the end of slavery.

Due to Booker's intense interest in learning, reading, and writing, his mother was able to get him a book. From this book, he was able to learn the alphabet and, eventually, to read and write. Legend has it that many times, Booker got up as early as four o'clock in the morning to study. He knew that once the day began, there would be little time for his educational pursuits.

In 1872, Booker heard about the Hampton-Normal Agricultural Institute in Hampton, Virginia. He was so interested in getting into that school that he walked five hundred miles to get to Hampton, Virginia. He did not complete the journey all at one time; he often worked wherever he could find work along the way.

Once he reached Hampton, he was able to reach the attention of the Hampton founder and president, General Samuel C. Armstrong, a black man who had been the commander and leader of a Union African American regiment during the Civil War. General Armstrong was dedicated to doing whatever he could to provide educational opportunities to newly freed black slaves. Booker T. Washington impressed this man so much that he offered this young, hardworking man a scholarship to Hampton. In 1875, Booker finished school at Hampton with high marks.

The first thing Booker did after graduating was return to his old school in Malden, West Virginia, to teach. After two years, General Armstrong asked Booker to come back to Hampton to teach. Booker T. became such a prominent educator that in 1881, the Alabama legislature approved a $2,000 grant for him to begin the Tuskegee Normal and Industrial School. The plan was not for Booker T. Washington to be the head of the school originally, but General Armstrong persuaded the people in the Alabama legislature to let Booker run the school.

The legislature listened to General Armstrong, and Booker T. Washington became the head of the Tuskegee school. The first classes were held in an old church building. When Booker took over, he spent much time traveling far and wide, raising money to continue the growth and praise of Tuskegee. The school went on to become Tuskegee Institute and is now Tuskegee University.

By the time Booker T. Washington died in 1915, Tuskegee had more than one hundred well-equipped buildings, more than fifteen hundred students, a faculty of over two hundred, the ability to teach at least thirty-eight trades and professions, and an endowment of over $2 million. And let us not forget that this was as early as 1915.

Lastly, this great African American man said, "I have learned that success is to be measured not so much by the position one has reached in life as by the obstacles he has had to overcome while trying to succeed."

Until you value yourself, you won't value your time. Until you value your time, you won't do anything with it.

—M. Scott Peck

CHAPTER 2

Why Go to School?

The idea of going to school as a requirement is built on a philosophy that began way back in antiquity. It is the philosophy of compulsory education. *Compulsory* refers to a period when it was declared that education was a requirement for every person. The idea goes back as early as Plato's *The Republic*. Even in ancient Judea, every parent was required to teach his or her children informally. Out of these ancient times and beliefs came the age of the rabbis. A Jewish man named Joshua ben Gamla is credited with starting the formal Jewish institutional education system in which every town was charged with having a school for children at the age of six or seven. Maybe this helps us understand why Jewish people have such adoration for being educated. Joshua ben Gamla's education system began in the first century AD.

The Aztec Triple Alliance, which ruled from 1428 to 1521 in what is now central Mexico, created the first state requiring universal compulsory education.

In the early modern era, Martin Luther, the German theologian and interpreter of the Bible, was a great advocate for compulsory education and schooling, because he wanted all his parishioners to have the ability to read the Bible for themselves. Strasbourg, a free city of the Holy Roman Empire, passed accordant legislation for compulsory education in the year 1508.

In Scotland, compulsory education became law through an act passed in 1633. In Prussia, a compulsory-education law was passed during the reign of Frederick the Great. In Australia and Hungary, the law became a reality in 1774, during the reign of Empress Maria Theresa.

The first state to pass a compulsory-education law in the United States was Massachusetts, in the year 1852. Similar laws spread rapidly to all of the other states, with the last state being Mississippi, in 1917. During this country's early years, education existed through church-run private schools. But a man named General Henry Pratt began laying the groundwork for compulsory education in the late 1800s. He wanted to provide educational opportunities to minorities across America in government-run schools. The prototype that General Pratt used was the Carlisle Indian Industrial School in Pennsylvania. Now in the United States, children are required to attend primary schools between the ages of six and twelve, and they attend junior or middle schools between the ages of twelve and fifteen. There are a few states where students can opt out of attending school between ages fourteen and seventeen.

—*ᑎᑎᑎ*—

The remaining pages of this chapter will contain commentary on why black children need to go to school and why they should want to go to school and have high expectations about their wish to go to school.

Once again, by the time your child has reached the age of two, he or she has reached a time when the concept of school is something he or she can begin to grasp. However, parents have to be sure to stress this idea often enough. The parent should be saying things like "When you start school," or "When you go to school." When children hear *school* often enough, their inquiring minds will ask, "What is school?" Then parents will be able to take the time to let their children know what school is. Parents then have the opportunity to begin explaining to these young children where they will be going in a few years.

Whatever explanation parents give, they should relay the information in a way that leads the children to look forward to school, rather than to feel dread or fear. They could say things like "You will have a lot of new friends," or "You will meet new playmates," or "It is a place where you will learn things and have fun at the same time." The only thing that is a real no-no is any kind of talking down about what children should expect at school.

You have an opportunity to get into your child's head so that he or she will look forward to going to some location five days per week and will view school as a pleasant experience. If you use some of the suggestions from the earlier chapter, such as acquainting your child with children's books and children's games and going to the library together, you will be doing yourself and your child a favor. You will have done what you needed to do in the way of steps for school preparation. It also would not hurt if you bought your child writing pads or tablets and pencils and crayons. Few little children do not like these early primary kinds of gifts.

Slowly, you introduce the concept that going to school is something that will be important for their future and something all children take part in. It also helps if parents tell children, in their own way, that once the school routine has begun, it is important to complete it all the way through high school at the very least. Parents know that public education is not a thing they must pay for, so there is no need to fret over elementary, middle, and high school being too expensive.

After the Sandy Hook shooting tragedy in Newton, Massachusetts, in mid-December 2012, I found it eye opening to listen to some six- and seven-year-old survivors speaking about the horrible event. They were able to express with such clarity and correctness and in such intelligent, understandable English different aspects of the senseless massacre. I mention this because it convinced me even more that I was on the right track regarding how much youngsters can learn when properly taught early on.

Another aspect of readiness for school is that children must learn early what discipline is. They must learn what proper discipline is and also realize that it is something they will need to accept. Teaching this lesson is again in the realm of the parents, who have the responsibility of doing their "homework" before their children venture out to classrooms. If done properly, parents should not have a lot of problems in teaching their children what is and is not proper behavior. Discipline involves a small amount of sternness but should not involve shouting at the child or cursing him or her.

Anyone reading this book, if honest, will have no problem admitting that too many of our children begin school with unresolved discipline. Unfortunately, young black boys are by and large much more problematic in class than other groups. When young individuals in a classroom are regularly disruptive or pay no attention to what their teacher is trying to teach, it makes for a bad situation not only for the teacher but also for those children who are disciplined and would like to learn.

At this point, I hope all parents of young children know what the concept of compulsory education is. Hopefully, if parents get young children motivated early to get up and go off to school five days per week to grow mentally, they will already be used to this kind of routine when they are no longer children. There is a connection between going to school and getting an education and later being knowledgeable enough to get a job and make a living. Compulsory education is not a concept that involves a child going away from home without a well-thought-out philosophy. When a pupil buys into the system, she or he, by the end of twelve years, will learn a lot, have a lot of self-confidence, and know that she or he will have a good chance of becoming successful in life.

Maybe the most important lesson parents and students alike should learn is that going to school and getting an education is a progressive thing. The system also involves what is known as meritocracy. Simply put, a meritocracy is a system that rewards perseverance. When a student remains in school long enough, he or she gets a high school diploma, which is the first important piece of academic paper one can earn. Graduating from kindergarten or middle school is just a nice gesture. Those diplomas are pieces of paper one can save, but no employer will be interested in seeing those if a child decides to drop out of school in the eighth or ninth grade.

Taking the meritocracy concept a bit further, we see that those who go on to complete two years of college (junior college) will be rewarded somewhat more than the high school graduate was. Those who persevere even more and go on to finish undergraduate college for a four-year degree will be rewarded with an even more important piece of paper: a bachelor's degree in some chosen field, called a major, usually with an accompanying minor. The college degree is the second-most-important piece of academic paper. I do not feel that it is necessary to go on about master's degrees and doctoral degrees. The point is that the system knows who to bestow the rewards upon. In short, in education, rewards go to those who are willing to work hard to acquire more and more education.

Chapter 2 Inspirational Choice

Dr. Benjamin Elijah Mays's Achievements

Chapter 2 had to do with the importance of education, as did chapter 1. For this reason, I chose another educational giant for the inspiration section following the chapter "Why Go to School?" As you will see, we have another African American who saw the light and realized that education was our pathway to success, progress, and prosperity.

Dr. Benjamin E. Mays was born in 1894. He lived an active life focused on attempting to make things better for African Americans. People thought of Dr. Mays mostly as an educator. However, he was also a renowned scholar and an activist for social justice for black people, and most recognized him as the most illustrious president of Morehouse College in Atlanta, Georgia. Morehouse continues to be the premier black men's college in America.

Dr. Mays was born in a small town called Ninety Six, South Carolina. He was the youngest of eight children. Like Booker T. Washington, he was a child born to parents who were former slaves. It is important for us to keep in mind what kind of odds these people faced. Yet they became some of the most recognized heroes of our race. It is also good to remember that these people had no problem seeing that the way to any eventual success was through education.

When Benjamin E. Mays was ready to go off to college, he spent his first year at Virginia Union University. After that first year, he transferred to Bates College in the state of Maine. Dr. Mays had such good grades that he was invited to come to Bates. He went on to receive his bachelor's degree from Bates and then went on to get a master's degree from the University of Chicago in 1925. Later, at the School of Religion at the University of Chicago, he received his doctorate of religion in 1935. After this, he went on to teach at Morehouse College and also at South Carolina State University.

In chapter 2, I mentioned how much one is rewarded in education based on the system of meritocracy. Dr. Mays understood that the more education and academic degrees one acquired, the more rewards he or she could receive. Dr. Mays seemed to never get enough education to satisfy him or his quest for knowledge.

By 1940, he was recognized and renowned enough to be chosen as the president of Morehouse College. One of the most rewarding things that happened to him at Morehouse was having a student by the name of Martin Luther King Jr. Martin became his favorite student of all time. Dr. Mays even delivered the eulogy for Martin in 1968, after Martin's assassination.

Dr. Benjamin Mays emphasized two major themes during his lifetime: one was the dignity of all human beings, and the other was the gap between American democratic ideals and American social practices. These ideals happened to be close to the elements Dr. Martin Luther King Jr. advocated during his civil rights movement.

Dr. Mays' most prominent book was *Seeking to be a Christian in Race Relations*, which was published in 1957. He also wrote a later book called *Born a Rebel*, published by Scribner in 1971. Dr. Mays retired from Morehouse in 1967. In 1982, the NAACP awarded him the Spingarn Medal, their highest award. Today there is a Benjamin E. Mays High School in Atlanta, and finally, Molefi Kete Asante listed him in *100 Greatest African Americans: A Biographical Encyclopedia* in 2002.

The Earth has music for those who listen.

—George Santayana

CHAPTER 3

From Then to the Present

Upon deciding to write about where we are as a race at this time in our history, I had to do some heavy pondering regarding how we got to the point where we now find ourselves. I thought about not only what happened but also, more importantly, why it happened. On the one hand, I can personally recall when things were a lot worse, and on the other hand, I can recall when we, as an ethic group, made better decisions than we are making currently. The worst was when blacks faced political dismissal and avid and open racism. African Americans faced more discrimination in just about everything. It was also worse in light of both the written laws and also the unwritten rules designed to diminish African Americans.

But on the other hand, we as a group were much better in the behavior we demonstrated. We were also much better at trying to access what it took for us to survive at a less-problematic level. We were better when it came to going to school. From what we saw, we knew that there were not going to be jobs around that one could do without at least a high school education, except something that was low paying or involved harsh, backbreaking menial labor. I guess I am saying that we understood things better back in those days. But now, for about two generations, our race has steadily sunk, as if in quicksand, to the point where we rank at the bottom or near the bottom of any positive statistic. Think about it. Call out some positives for yourself, or to someone else, and see what answers you will get on a scale from one to ten, with ten being the highest or best.

For that reason, I felt the need to do some serious research on where this falling back began. I think I might have a good grasp of where it began, even if I find it hard to give an accurate account of why it began. I would like to give you a bit of a hint. Things got better for us in the way of laws and pathways for upward movement and mobility, but at the same time, two generations of backsliding among our race began.

So in essence, this chapter will be one in which I present historical evidence from the mid-1950s to the end of the Lyndon B. Johnson presidency. I will present a series of events that we can look at historically as an age of improvements for black people. One thing for sure is that we were not losing ground during those years, from 1954 to 1967.

The series of events that took place were as follows:

1. *Brown v. the Board of Education* (1954)

2. The start of Dr. Martin L. King Jr.'s civil rights activism movement under the name SCLC (Southern Christian Leadership Conference), sparked by the Rosa Parks back-of-the-bus incident in Montgomery, Alabama (1955)

3. The election of John F. Kennedy as the first Catholic president (1960)

4. The assassination of President Kennedy during the last year of his only term (1963)

5. The birth of other civil rights groups, such as SNCC (Student Nonviolent Coordination Committee) and CORE (Congress of Racial Equality), all were developed by 1960

6. The start of Vice President Lyndon B. Johnson's presidency after the death of President Kennedy in November 1963

7. President Johnson's pledge to carry out the Kennedy wish for a war on poverty immediately upon coming into office in 1963

8. President Johnson's success in passing the Civil Rights Act in 1964, during the first year of his presidency

9. President Johnson's success in getting the Voting Rights Act passed in 1965

10. President Johnson's wish to pursue his own dream, which was called "the Great Society"

Over the thirteen years from 1954 until the end of President Johnson's reign as president of the United States in 1967, each of the ten events listed above helped make life better for African Americans. So my task now is to go into some more detailed explanations as to how everything on the list had some direct impact on the future of black people in America.

Brown v. the Board of Education

White segregationists, almost exclusively in the South, who were the greatest advocates of keeping the Jim Crow way of doing things alive, had come up with laws based on the idea of "separate but equal." Everyone, white or black, understood that these laws were tactics to keep the races from being together and also to keep an advantage for whites.

One of the greatest flaws and fallacies in the separate-but-equal argument involved what was going on in the schools in the South. When lawmakers spoke of separate but equal in schools, it was a downright farce. Because of the compulsory-education rules and laws in the country, all cities and towns had to provide some kind of education for all children when they reached the age of six years old. Under the separate-but-equal mentality, cities provided a school—or maybe two elementary schools—that was not equal to what the Caucasians had for their children. Most of the ramshackle buildings the black children attended were dilapidated wood-frame buildings. The books they used for their education were older books that the white children had previously used. Some books did not even have back covers on them or had torn or missing pages. Further, many of these elementary schools placed two grades in the same classroom; one grade was on one side of the room, and the other was on the opposite side. The same teacher was to teach both grades.

After elementary school, there was an even greater void in black education, as towns in the South did not provide high schools for blacks. They figured that they had satisfied the compulsory-school laws by providing schools that went through the sixth or seventh grade. This arrangement turned out to be just a few steps from the days of slavery. As I mentioned when discussing Booker T. Washington, back in the days of slavery, it was illegal for blacks to learn to read. We can figure out from common sense that the Jim Crow whites wanted to keep blacks as close to slavery as possible.

However, the case of *Brown v. the Board of Education* was a major move upward for black people, particularly black pupils, which recognized that as things were, there was no "separate but equal" in the schools where the races were not sitting in the same classrooms.

The most widely covered event coming out of this decision was the ruling that Central High School in Little Rock, Arkansas, had to be integrated. To make that happen, President Dwight D. Eisenhower had to deploy the National Guard to Little Rock to get the so-called Little Rock Nine into the school on the first day.

I cannot understand how anyone could fail to see that this case was a major advantage for black people. When in our history, in this racist and hostile country, had we ever before had a major court decision end up on our side? When had we ever seen the National Guard called out by an American president to uphold a law that came down on our side?

Dr. Martin L. King Jr. Beginning His Civil Rights Movement and the SCLC (Southern Christian Leadership Conference)

We see a street named Martin L. King Jr. Drive in just about every major city in this country, and even in not-so-major cities. We also have a holiday dedicated to the mammoth work Dr. King did in attempting to make things better for African American people. In fact, he died in his efforts to make things better for us. At the time of his assassination in 1968, he had moved to recognition of not just civil rights but also the equally important field of human rights.

Dr. King came to the decision to go all out for civil rights after the disrespectful way Ms. Rosa Parks was treated on a Montgomery, Alabama, bus. Once he got started, he never turned back in his efforts to make things better for black people. He even went to jail for civil obedience a few times. His most celebrated jail time was when he was incarcerated in a Birmingham jail, where he wrote his now-famous letter. From the brilliant ideas conceived by Dr. King, based largely on the pacifism and nonviolence concepts of Mahatma Gandhi, other black organizations were formed. Two of the others were SNCC (Student Nonviolent Coordinating Committee) and CORE (Congress of Racial Equality). As far as black people doing things to try to help themselves, these were some of our finest hours and finest years. Because of Reverend King, there were many black churches and black church members involved. SNCC involved the participation of many young black people and students. It seemed at the time that our race was going to get somewhere at last.

John F. Kennedy Elected as First Catholic President

When John F. Kennedy was campaigning for the presidency before 1960, it was a time kind of like when Barack Obama was campaigning to become the first black president. Kennedy eventually defeated Richard M. Nixon. He went on to be a sympathizer with Dr. King and his goals and ideals. John Kennedy was tremendously popular with black people because we could all see the genuine feelings he had for our downtrodden plight as a group of people who had to try to survive under hatred and misery in a country we had been dragged to and then built as slaves. There are still speculations that Kennedy being Catholic and also on the same page with Dr. King was a large part of the conspiracy that led to his assassination.

Vice President Lyndon B. Johnson Becoming President

President Kennedy was shot to death in a successful assassination attempt in Dallas, Texas. His vice president was a former senator from Texas. Some wild rumors circulated after the president was shot to death, including a rumor that the vice president had some part in the assassination plot, the wildest reason being so that he could become president.

However, those of us who had the privilege of watching Lyndon B. Johnson sworn in as president heard him say the words "I will do the best that I can. That is all that I can do." It remained to be seen if these were empty words or if he was genuine. After all, Johnson was a Democrat from Texas, and at that time, all of the southerners were Democratic. That being so, the Dixiecrats, as people called them then, felt they had it made with one of their own at the helm. But their hopes were short-lived

To the amazement of both black people, who felt their hopes and dreams had perished with the death of President Kennedy, and the southern white Democratic senators and congressmen, Lyndon Johnson surprised everybody. After Kennedy's death in the last year of his term, Lyndon Johnson was automatically now the president. The next election would be coming up in 1964, and that was going to be President Johnson's election to win or lose. The surprise was that he went right ahead and announced that he wanted to be sure to carry out a goal of late President Kennedy and start a war on poverty. This was a bold move for a southern Dixiecrat ex-senator from Texas. Black people could breathe sighs of relief. Johnson was savvy enough to know that he would be overwhelmingly getting the black vote in the 1964 election.

President Johnson went on to get reelected in the 1964 race for president. He shocked everyone even more by getting the Civil Rights Act passed during his first year in office. He went on to get the Voting Rights Act passed in 1965. Black people did not believe a southerner was doing all these good things for them. But he did not stop there. President Johnson wanted to carve out a title plan of his own. Most of what he had done was carry out what John Kennedy had hoped to achieve.

President Johnson was ready to go much further than anyone could have imagined. The program that would be his own was a hope for the fall of 1965. That program was his Great Society announcement. President Johnson first mentioned his Great Society plan in the May 22, 1964, Michigan University commencement address he gave, which is purported to have been the largest commencement ever. There were 4,973 graduates, plus faculty, parents, and others. It was there that the president spoke of his Great Society plan. But the Great Society never really got off the ground, as President Johnson became more and more weighed down by the complications of the Vietnam War. Because of that weight, which he felt he could not bear, he decided not to run for election again in 1968.

—⁓—

In summary, the passage of the Civil Rights Act of 1964 was monumental. It formally dismantled the Jim Crow system of discrimination in public accommodations, rules of employment, voting, education, and federally financed activities.

It's baffling that we did not gain further success after all that happened during these years. Many of us rushed through the door when these weights were lifted. But the most puzzling part is this: What caused so many who came to the fork in the road of the era to choose the wrong path? It's a shame that we have not been at the top of anything positive since then, and we have been the lowest in many positive stats. On the other hand, we appear at or near the top on a list of anything considered negative.

—❦—

Brown v. the Board of Education is just part of the name of the court case. The complete name is *Brown v. the Board of Education of Topeka*. This case was an important case for black people, and in the end, we did not lose it. It was one of the most important legal decisions that has ever come out in favor of black mobility, against black injustice through segregation, and in favor of black upward movement in education.

There was a fiftieth-anniversary celebration of *Brown v. the Board of Education* in 2004. It should have been a joyous celebration and occasion, but it did not quite turn out that way. It's important to note what statistics available fifty years after this momentous decision have found. Without further ado, here are the findings.

1. Black people make up 13 percent of the nation's population, but in 2003 (just one year before this fiftieth gala), the nation's prison population was 44 percent black. One out of every ten black men between the ages of twenty-five and twenty-nine was in prison.

2. In 2004, federal data showed that black Americans still made up just 13 percent of the population but accounted

for 37 percent of violent crimes, 54 percent of arrests for robberies, and 51 percent of murders.

3. The majority of these murders were murders of other blacks.

4. At the start of the fifties, 65 percent of inmates in all state and federal prisoners were white. At the time, only 35 percent were black.

5. By the end of the century, the white prison population had declined to 35 percent, while the black prison population had risen to 50 percent.

6. A statistical model done in the 1990s concluded that a low-income black man born in 2001 had a 33 percent chance of going to prison during his lifetime.

7. At the end of 2003, 10 percent of black males between the ages of twenty-five and twenty-nine were in prison.

8. In an op-ed piece written for the *Los Angeles Times* in June of 2004, Bill Cosby wrote that he had statistics showing that there was a 50 percent dropout rate and a 60 percent illiteracy rate among the prison population, which was 45 percent black.

So there we have it. It is sad for African Americans to have such an important case decided in our favor but not take advantage of what the court handed to us back in 1954. *Brown v. the Board of Education* wiped out what Jim Crow stood for. I can attest personally that this victory resulted in an upgrade in educational endeavors for black people and pupils.

To wrap up this chapter, I want to say that we are not going to get anywhere quickly if all we can come up with is that our people, mostly the young men, are trapped in the ghetto, do not have the facilities or other things they need in poor schools, or are too much into poverty to get out. We—black people—need to admit that this is nothing more than just another - "hold ourselves back" - excuse.

My first question, in light of the gift we received when we won the *Brown v. the Board* trial, is "Trapped in the ghetto by what?" Do they not, today, have unrestricted access to schools where they can go and get an education? As Tina Turner said in one of her biggest hits, "What's love got to do with it?" In this case, what's poverty got to do with it? We can still learn as much as we need to or want to no matter how poor we are. Why was Booker T. Washington, an ex-slave, not hindered from becoming one of the greatest learners and, eventually, greatest educators despite the abject poverty and cruelty he was born into?

As I stated earlier, we are going to have to get to the point where we are ready to shed this dead skin of excuse after excuse regarding why we are not able to make any real gains in our race as far as moving forward rather than backward. The lame excuses are not enough anymore in the larger public and American society.

When we get down to the real truth, our race is not ever going to be worth much until we decide that the way up is education. Our black parents must stop eschewing education and tell their children that without some adequate educational competency, they will be living unsuccessful lives.

Too many black parents do not seem to respect the power of education. Their children can easily pick up on that attitude. And when that happens, there goes another black generation into the garbage pits of ignorance and failure.

Chapter 3 Inspirational Choice

The Achievements of Justice Thurgood Marshall

Thurgood Marshall was born in the city of Baltimore in 1908. His parents were born after the end of slavery and just before the beginning of the Jim Crow era. Thurgood's parents taught him to be a proud person and to respect the rewards that were possible through education. His father was a dining steward at an all-white private club. His mother was a grade-school teacher.

Thurgood attended Baltimore's Douglas High School. He went on to attend Lincoln University in Oxford, Pennsylvania. He earned great respect as a scholar while at Lincoln University and graduated with honors in 1930. He left Lincoln and entered Howard University Law School. The University of Maryland had denied him admission for the obvious reason of the time: all-white colleges and universities did not allow black students in the 1930s. However, his denial from Maryland University worked out well for him. At Howard, he had the pleasure of getting to know the vice dean, Charles H. Houston. This man became a mentor for Thurgood as he went on to graduate magna cum laude from Howard in 1933.

As fate would have it, Dr. Charles H. Houston was the first chief counsel for the NAACP. Dr. Houston invited Thurgood to come to work with him at the NAACP, and when he left, Thurgood was a natural to replace him as chief counsel. After he moved into the NAACP's top position, the rest was history, as Justice Marshall became more successful and recognized as a brilliant attorney, especially in winning big civil rights cases.

In a 1992 interview with the American Bar Association, Thurgood said Dr. Houston impressed upon him that a good lawyer is a lawyer who strives to be a "social engineer." Long before Justice Marshall was appointed to the Supreme Court as the first African American, he had a résumé that included not only arguing many signature cases but also winning these cases. He had spoken out many times against *Plessy v. Ferguson*, an 1896 ruling that predated *Brown v. the Board of Education*. It was similar because *Plessy v. Ferguson* was also a discrimination ruling in which the major tenets had to do with the idea of separate but equal. As Howard Ball wrote in his article *'Thurgood's Coming' - Tale of a Hero Lawyer* (Jackson Free Press - 5/12/2004) - Thurgood Marshall believed "so long as Plessy was in the law books, so long as it was 'bright letter' law on the subject of equality of the races, blacks and other minorities would forever be second-class citizens."

Justice Marshall had already argued against an unfair housing statute in *Sweatt v. Painter* in 1948 and had won that case. Before President Johnson appointed him to the Supreme Court, Thurgood served as chief counsel on *Brown v. the Board of Education*, which was his most important case, because of all of the barriers it brought down in discrimination against black people.

In 1967, during the last year of the Lyndon B. Johnson presidency, the president offered up the name of Thurgood Marshall to become the first African American Supreme Court justice. The opening came about when Justice Tom Clark retired. Thurgood had to endure several days of brutal questioning, mostly from Senator Sam Ervin Jr. of North Carolina. But in the end, only a smattering of diehard southerners voted against his confirmation.

It is important to note that prior to his Supreme Court appointment, Justice Marshall had the distinction of bringing thirty-two cases before the Supreme Court. He won twenty-nine of those cases. Before leaving the Supreme Court, and before his death in 1993 at the age of eighty-five, he was asked how he would wish to be remembered. The justice said, "I would like to be remembered for having done the best I could with what I had."

How much better our race would be today, and the world, if all of us adopted that kind of attitude.

The only power to which man should aspire is that which he exercises over himself

—Ellie Wiesel

CHAPTER 4

What Ever Happened to Stigma?

The *Webster New World Dictionary* gives six definitions for *stigma.*[2] Three of them are germane to this discussion: (1) "A distinguishing mark burned or cut into the flesh, as a slave or criminal," (2) "Something that detracts from the character or reputation of a person or group, etc.; mark of disgrace or reproach," and (3) "A mark, sign, etc., indicating that something is not considered normal or standard."

All three definitions have to do with something that rises to a recognizable level and becomes a public shame.

Because a stigma is an issue or thing that rises to the level of public shame, a stigma is serious enough to defame or do harm to the reputation of an entire group—in this instance, black individuals.

In life, it is necessary for one to learn to take advantage of opportunities. To do so, a person has to learn how to recognize an opportunity whenever one becomes available. For all of us, being able to go to school is, without question, one of the greatest opportunities that America has to offer, especially because we all have the ability to gain an education for free.

We all need to have sense enough to realize that everything worthwhile has an already-defined structure. We need to

---

[2] *Webster New World Dictionary*, 3rd ed. (New York: Simon and Schuster, 1988).

relentlessly follow everything that has a defined discipline. We need to remind ourselves and understand that the discipline already in place, if followed the proper way, will eventually lead to a successful life path. Most of the time, when a person opts to leave the proven, workable discipline track, that person is headed for trouble—if not real trouble, they are at least veering off onto a pathway that will not be fully rewarding to them in the way of happiness, contentment, or financial stability as they proceed through life. Parents need to understand such a success track and present it to children when they are young. That is not to say that the children will understand it immediately, but they will understand at some point if parents tell them enough times what is needed from them. They will see that following a successful path is a habit they will form, and it will be easy to form and to follow. Getting committed to good, sensible daily habits is one of the best things for young children to learn to ensure that they can live lives of contentment and reasonable comfort.

A simple example of a good track would be understanding the opportunities inherent in learning to read and write and also understanding the opportunities of becoming a regular visitor to the library and discovering the wonders there. This leads one to the opportunities that will be inherent in being serious about wanting to attend school and, after going to school, being serious about wanting to do well while there. Then comes an understanding of the importance of forming good morals and good character at an early age through religious instruction. You want the child grounded early in what things are right and what things are wrong. Put another way, children must learn which things to move toward and which things to avoid or back away from. Another good thing about churches is that there is no black community in which churches are hard to find.

All of the things I have stated above can prepare us to get more into the theory or philosophy of stigma. The first kind of stigma is institutional stigma. This can come about if you get branded as a felon in the criminal-justice system. You can even be out of prison and on parole or probation, and still be unable to vote or do jury service, because you get branded with the label of being a second-class citizen. That is the figurative scar or brand mentioned in the first definition above.

Michelle Alexander, in *The New Jim Crow*, speaks of how Frederick Douglass and other delegates attended the National Colored Convention in Rochester, New York, in the summer of 1853. They were there to discuss the condition, status, and future of coloreds. They decried the stigma of race—the scorn heaped upon blacks for no other reason than their skin color. They held this convention before the beginning of the Civil War and, of course, before the end of slavery. Most of the delegates were able to attend because they were freed slaves, and a few young people who had been born free also attended.

There are questions that we need to honestly ask ourselves as African Americans today. We also need to try to be honest in giving ourselves the answers.

The questions are these: Are too many black individuals doing too many negative things at this point in time? And are we doing things that stigmatize us beyond the stigma we face because of the color of our skin?

Here is a list you can ponder.

1. Today's statistics show that more African Americans are in prison than any other race.

2. Statistics show that more African Americans drop out of school.

3. African Americans have the highest rate of unemployment. That is to be expected, if we choose not to persevere and remain in school to get an education. At minimum, we need a high school education to get most lower-level jobs.

4. Statistics show that black men often fail to financially take care of the children they were a part of bringing into the world.

5. Within our race, most of the out-of-wedlock births were freed slaves who were children of slave owners. A few involved young people who had been born free.

6. African Americans are the worst when it comes to gang membership, and we also kill more of our own than any other race each year.

7. We lately have voluntarily chosen to see how bad we can look and dress in terms of our public appearance. We do not take pride in trying to see how good or dignified we can look, especially young black males.

8. At this time, too many of our young black males feel it is easier to pursue a career in pushing drugs than to take the necessary steps to get a real, legal job. They are also the ones who want to protest when they wind up in jail. They want to protest further when they come out of jail with a ruined life, brought about by their own choices.

After reading the above list, we can see how African Americans are still stigmatized, but not just because of the color of our skin. We might take a little time to wonder what Frederick Douglass and the other delegates who attended the National Colored Convention in 1853 would say if they were able to see some of the backward, negative behavior we present today. What would they say if they could see the myriad opportunities we now have at our disposal—opportunities we are failing in droves to take advantage of? The chapter's title asked the following question: "What ever happened to stigma?" The answer is that stigmas are still part of African American culture. However, we must admit that the stigmas are no longer all due to racism and the color of our skin. The actions and behaviors of too many of us are keeping the negative stereotypes alive and well.

Chapter 4 Inspirational Choice

Congresswoman Shirley St. Anita Chisholm

Ms. Chisholm was born as Shirley St. Anita Hill Chisholm in Brooklyn, New York, in 1924. She was the oldest of four girls born to West Indian immigrants. Her family was barely able to exist off the meager earnings her father made while working in a factory and also doing house cleaning.

When Shirley was three years old, her parents sent her and her other sisters to their maternal grandmother in Barbados in an attempt to find a better way for the children. As fate would have it, Shirley liked the island of Barbados. There was an excellent school and educational system in place using the British system in Barbados. For many years, black people in the United States were able to feel a special kind of pride for Barbados. It was hailed as one of the countries, if not the country, with the highest rate of literacy. Over 90 percent of the people in Barbados were able to read and write.

Shirley was ten years old when she returned to Brooklyn. Back in Brooklyn, she continued to be an outstanding student. This led to her having the smarts to be able to enter Brooklyn College. At Brooklyn College, she majored in sociology. She also joined the debate team. On the debate team, she gained important experience that would serve in developing her cut-and-thrust oratory style.

After her graduation from Brooklyn College, her thirst for knowledge and further education took her to night classes at Columbia University in New York City. She graduated from Brooklyn College in 1949 and started taking night classes at Columbia. At Columbia, she eventually earned a master's degree in childhood education. In the meantime, Shirley taught at a nursery school in Harlem. She later served as a supervisor of the largest nursery school network in the city of New York.

Through her administrative experience, she gained executive skills that would later serve her well in the political arena. In 1953, she became a key member of the Seventh Assembly District Democratic Club. She would go on to wage a successful political campaign to help elect an eminent black lawyer to the municipal court of New York.

In 1964, her own political career took off when she won a landslide victory in her campaign for a seat in the New York State Assembly. As an assemblywoman (1965–1968), she wrote the legislation that established what would become known as SEEK (Search for Education Elevation and Knowledge). This program was designed to help provide college funding for promising but disadvantaged black youth.

Ms. Chisholm's fame and brilliance eventually led her to become the first African American woman elected to the Congress of the United States. She also had the distinction of becoming the first woman to campaign for the presidency of the United States. Shirley Chisholm was for Jesse Jackson when he became a candidate for the presidency.

When she became a congressperson in 1968, she served on several committees, including Education and Labor, and she also campaigned vigorously for a higher minimum wage. In 1972, she began her campaign that would pave the way for other African Americans to have visions of one day becoming president of the United States of America.

In 1973, she wrote an autobiography titled *The Good Fight*. She retired from Congress in 1982 but remained an active political figure in the area of education.

There is one quote in particular that she is remembered for. In a speech before the Congressional Black Caucus in Washington in 1966, she said, "I am so tired of us being a race that is so proud of being a poor race." That statement made many at the caucus, and many not at the caucus, do a bit more thinking before talking about how poor we were and how impotent we were because of poverty.

Above and beyond the stellar accomplishments I already mentioned, Ms. Chisholm garnered many other coveted awards and notable recognitions for her excellent lifetime service for our race. She passed away in the year 2005.

The only lies for which we are truly punished are those we tell ourselves.

—V. S. Naipaul

CHAPTER 5

The Plight of the Young Black Female

I want to begin this chapter by telling the young black females of our race thank you for being the least of our current problems. I have purposely aimed this chapter at the young black female, as our older women are not so much a part of what I need to say here. Their job was being good parents to those young females who are now between the ages of fifteen and thirty. My saying that these young black females are the least of the problems does not mean there are no important issues to discuss and address. There are important issues that we need to discuss and address—issues that can help us, as a race, make some significant moves up and away from the bottom of the negative barrel in which we now find ourselves.

There are three concerns that I hope black young women will seriously consider. First, I hope they can do whatever they need to do to respect themselves. Second, I hope they will see the value of always doing whatever they need to do to demand respect for themselves from others. Lastly, I hope they will be able to discern and to make wise decisions regarding what will affect their future well-being.

As I am writing this book in 2013, it is common—and has been for a long time—for black young women to go it alone as mothers. They have also found themselves having to be more responsible than should be necessary as the breadwinners.

37

For all of the above reasons, I will dedicate this chapter to young black females and their status in the midst of the African American problems surrounding them and the rest of us.

I think we need to first focus on the issue of respecting oneself. I grew up at a time much different from what we see and hear on a daily basis now. That was a time when black people were honestly trying to show a better side and attempting to shed our race of the stigma placed on our people out of hatred and racism.

Much to my dismay, today there seems to be a pervasive attitude of "I really don't care what people think or say about me." I am referring to young black females being used in videos where they are scantily clad and gyrating in poses that are the same as being in the act of sexual intercourse. That means they are complicit with, and affirm, the awful names that black male rappers call them. More clearly, they are not showing respect for themselves. There are also young black females who wear low-rider jeans or pants that allow everyone to see their thongs or panties. Some have on no underwear, and in those instances, everyone can clearly see a few inches of their cracks. According to the latest craze, young black women go outside in public wearing their pajama bottoms. As I write this, that low-life craze is still picking up speed.

When young black females exhibit the above behavior, they seem to be saying, "I do not respect myself." They also have no respect for themselves when they pay $100 or more to go to some venue to listen to gangsta rappers put them down by spouting misogynistic messages full of vulgarities, calling them female dogs and everything else that is low-life. But the females in the audience are jumping up and down and screaming with delight with their hands up in the air. They seem to be saying, "We love being called disrespectful names." Go figure.

Further, when it comes to the area of demanding respect, there is a clear void in the behavior of many black females. On any day, one can go out into the street and see a young black lady walking along beside a young black male who has his pants falling off. In some instances, the boy's pants are so far down that he has to constantly hold on to his pants at the zipper or button area so that he can walk. The point is that the young black female walking along with him becomes as much of an object of derision as he is. It is clear that she is not demanding respect. Some black people, who should have much more common sense, say, "Oh, it's just a fashion fad." Walking around with your pants falling off and your shorts showing is just another fashion fad? When did something so ugly and vulgar rise to the point where the word *fashion* could be used? We have a nation full of young black men who are now more impressed with how people wear clothing inside prisons than how they should dress in public or inside a classroom.

Young women, you are going along with a bunch of low-class stuff that you could help erase if you had any dedication to erasing it. You could simply say, "I am not going to walk down the street with you looking like you are, with your pants falling off. That's disrespectful to me." If enough of you would take this measure, you can bet that a lot of pants would be worn properly again in a relatively short period of time. You should ask yourself, "What is it I am hoping to gain in the long run by walking along with, dating, or whatever a young male person who has this kind of daily mind-set?"

We can now move on to the out-of-wedlock issue. I have to say at the beginning of this discussion that there are black women who have gone past the adolescent or teenage years and have become accomplished enough to have their feet firmly planted on the ground. These women likely have had enough time to discern that they would like to fulfill their female desires to have a child or children. However, they are doing this with the knowledge that they do not want to enter any kind of legal situation with black men who will only be major problems for them in the not-too-distant future. That considered, they make decisions to have children out of wedlock and also know that they will be able to take care of their children. That type of black female can carry on. She has understood that most black men today are already married, in prison, on parole, or gay. None of these is a safe bet for marriage, because down the road, she will have on her plate the burden of taking care of the child, him, and everything else that needs to be taken care of where money is concerned. These are the guys who feel they are slick enough to never have to work. They feel that they can always find a way to never have to work. It is good for young women to keep this in mind—that this was these men's reasoning when they decided to drop out of school. They felt there was no way they needed to continue to go to school. They could always find a female who would be swept away by their swag or charm, and they would have it made for life. So these women who have the means to go their way without needing one of these black males are exceptions.

Now we get to the out-of-wedlock problem. A 2004 statistic placed black out-of-wedlock births at 69.2 percent in 2004. The out-of-wedlock birth rate at the time was 45 percent for Hispanics and 24.5 percent for whites. In 2007, the out-of-wedlock birth rate for blacks was at 70 percent.

The major problem with teenage pregnancies of black females is that these are girls, not women. They will more than likely be young girls who are not going to ever have help from the father(s). They are also young girls who should still be in school, and they have no idea what it means to be a mother or what the daily routine of a mother should be. The most devastating statistic shows that in financial terms, the young black single mother is among the poorest women in America.

Getting back to the matter of knowing how to be discerning, one has to wonder what is in a black female's mind when she allows herself to become pregnant by a male she clearly knows, based on all of the evidence and knowledge available to her, has little chance of ever being financially successful. And if he did become successful financially, he would not be a person to count on, due to personality deficits and a propensity toward domestic violence. One of the saddest things about young women getting pregnant is that they are not educated and also know little of what is involved in the child-raising daily regime.

Back in 2004, when Bill Cosby made all-out efforts to talk to black people about how bad our race was looking when compared to other races, others severely criticized him. Today we can see how much better off we would be if Bill Cosby had been listened to. Later, Juan Williams wrote a book with the title *Enough*. In that book, he talks about Cosby a lot. He agreed with what Cosby had tried to make clear. One of the questions he asks in the book is "Where is the critical revulsion at the greed from the likes of BET in electronically exploiting black women?"

There are many warnings for low-income single mothers to take more responsibility in being aware that their young children do not need to see them consistently bringing strange men into the house. There are also messages that these young mothers need to take all precautions necessary in not letting their young daughters hear them having sex. That is important because exposure to sex too early can become the beginning of the rearing of yet another generation of out-of-wedlock pregnancies. Parents must teach their children, especially their daughters, that this is not the way to go; rather, they should get an education.

When it comes to gangster rap, the major themes are sex and violence. If you listen carefully, you'll find that there is a total disregard for women in the ways of warmth, feelings, and compassion. This genre is all about the black male, and he is in his head. Through their bragging, rappers are brainwashing young black females to think they are the greatest. As black people, we can speak about the harm of gangster rappers—yet they are still adored. Fans say, "Yeah, but they are making a lot of big money." That is the most harmful thing of all. Through minstrels, white money-loving people are destroying us as a race via the worst representatives of our race: vulgar, ignorant, profanity-loving, ranting, misogynistic young idiots. The more our young women and not-so-young women buy into this nothing-positive rap, the worse we will continue to be as a race.

It is important for young black women to realize that when they are entering relationships with young black males who have become so enraptured with the philosophy of rappers, there is no love there. What they do is cash in on what they see in the young girl who has been suckered in to the gangster rap. She is then just a helpless and hopeless young thing for others to prey upon. She does not really understand that these young black rappers have duped her into thinking they are great. They have a lot of money, but they do not have any common sense. They also don't care how much they are helping the racist and white establishment bring us to our knees as a race. Their white benefactors love paying them to destroy us. What could be more gratifying to them than to see every other young black male drop out of school, ape the prison culture in the way they dress, and eventually commit a crime and go to prison? Mission accomplished!

When a young black female goes along with the program, she becomes another one of those single mothers. Much too late, she realizes that what she bought into has ruined all of her chances to have a good, successful life. At this point, she realizes she is a highly uneducated woman who has a child and will never have an opportunity to go to college. She has little opportunity to get any well-paying employment, because her chance for success is now gone.

Young black women who give birth without the legality of marriage need to realize that people will forever refer to them as unwed mothers. The part that is unfair is that people never refer to the young men who help bring these children into the world as unwed fathers. That stigma of *unwed* still falls on the female. This is probably the most essential thing black females have to get a grip on: if you must have sex, do not do so in a way in which you cannot prevent yourself from becoming pregnant. If you must have a child, why do you feel the need to do so before you reach the age of adulthood? Why do you feel that you need to have a child when you are still a child? This is the kind of bad decision that too many black teens make. The result is that they ruin their lives.

To end this chapter, I need to mention a recent article in the *New York Daily News*. In the article, Planned Parenthood blasted the mayor for a city-sponsored ad speaking out against teen pregnancy. These ads appeared on subways and at city bus shelters. They had pictures of black babies pondering different issues, such as what would happen to them, what they would do if the dad left, and what their chances were of graduating from high school.

According to where you are on the issue, either the ad makes sense, or you will be against it. The *Daily News* reported last month that this tactic appeared to be working. Teen pregnancy dropped 27 percent over the last decade, as the number of teens having sex fell, and the proportion using birth control rose.

A spokeswoman for the Bloomberg administration said, "This city has been a national leader in allocating resources to make birth control available, and provide sex education to young people, but at the same time we must send a strong message that teen pregnancy has consequences—and those consequences are extremely negative, life-altering and most often disproportionately borne by young women."

I can only say in ending this chapter that I concur wholeheartedly with what spokeswoman Sarah Levine said. These young black women will a lot of the time give birth but definitely should not be dropping out of school to rush the experience.

Chapter 5 Inspirational Choice

Barbara Charline Jordan

Ms. Barbara Jordan was the first woman to be elected as a state senator in the State of Texas. She was also, later, the first southern black woman to serve in the United States Congress. Over time, Ms. Jordan became known as one of the most spellbinding orators of all time.

Barbara Jordan was born in 1936. She was the youngest daughter of three, born to Benjamin and Arlyne (Patten) Jordan. The father was a part-time minister and also a warehouse laborer. The family resided in one of the predominantly black districts of Houston, Texas. This district was known as the fifth ward.

Barbara Jordan attended Houston's Phyllis Wheatley High School. She was an exemplary student. She joined the debate team and won many awards, including the National Usher's Oratorical Prize. By the year 1953, she had made up her mind to become a lawyer. Immediately after graduating from high school, she enrolled in the historically black Texas Southern University. While there, she majored in government. With the help and guidance of her debate coach, Tom Freeman, she polished her oratorical skills even more. She became such a great debater and orator that she was able to persuade Mr. Freeman to include her on what had been the all-male traveling debate team. This happened despite the coach's policy of never taking any women on the national tours.

It just so happened that Ms. Jordan was entering college as the *Board of Education* case was heard. This case would end the federal tolerance of segregation in US educational institutions. After the judges ruled in favor of blacks and other minorities, Barbara Jordan traveled all over the United States with debating teams. National female debaters had never been allowed prior to 1954. Ms. Jordan became one of the African

Americans to gain a tie in a debate with white debaters from Harvard University.

Upon her graduation from Texas Southern University, Ms. Jordan decided to further her education by enrolling at Boston University Law School. In 1956, Barbara found herself one of two black women who were part of a freshman class of six hundred. Within months of graduating from law school, she returned to Houston. She had determined that she wanted a career in politics. She volunteered as a worker on the Kennedy and Johnson presidential campaign team in 1960. It was not long before other white campaigners were taking notice of this black woman who had such a great talent for public speaking. She was readily picked up to go on the speech-making circuit for the Harris County Democrats.

Ms. Jordan was now ready to use her widespread popularity to campaign for her own job. She lost her first two runs for the Texas senate in 1962. However, in 1966, she won her senate seat by a margin of two to one over a popular white liberal.

In 1972, Ms. Jordan decided to run for a national position and was elected to the House of Representatives. She became a member of the Judiciary Committee and received national recognition for her moving indictment of President Richard Nixon during the Watergate hearings. She was smart as a politician. She never gained a reputation for being a radical or confrontational in her politics. She once made the following statement: "I am neither a black politician nor a female politician—just a politician."

By 1979, Ms. Jordan had decided to retire from Congress, largely because she had become afflicted with multiple sclerosis. Once again, she returned to Texas and taught public policy at the Lyndon B. Johnson School of Public Affairs. From 1970 to 1996, she continued to devote herself to public service, and she was chosen to give the keynote speech at the Democratic National Convention in 1992. Later, she served as chair of the US Commission on Immigration Reform.

Before Ms. Jordan's death in 1996, she earned more awards than I can list here, including the prestigious Eleanor Roosevelt Humanities Award in 1984. She received more than twenty honorary doctorates from leading US universities. She also wrote a book, *Barbara Jordan: A Self-Portrait.*[3]

She was yet another African American who was not born into any kind of wealth and faced all kinds of open racism and segregation during her lifetime. But Ms. Jordan, like many other blacks who rose to greatness, refused to let the obstacles that could have gotten in her way hold her back. She was a famous and successful person who serves as another shining example for both women and men.

---

[3] Barbara Jordan, *Barbara Jordan: A Self-Portrait* (New York: Doubleday and Company, 1979).

You cannot find peace by avoiding life.

—Virginia Woolf

CHAPTER **6**

The Plight of the Young—and Not-So-Young—African American Male

This chapter will probably get more African Americans angry with me than any of the others. So be it. My purpose for writing this book was to express many realizations and get them off my chest. So let's get started by going back to the cavemen. They were the hunters, providers, and breadwinners (maybe meat winners would be more appropriate)—the people in their families who took on most of the tasks that kept their families together and surviving. For the Native Americans in America, it was the young brave who provided for and protected the young maidens and female squaws. And in terms of the "lowly" animals that we are supposed to have so much more intelligence than, the male of every species is the hunter, provider, and protector of his territory and his family in that staked-out territory.

Now let us move to the current times. What other ethnicity can any of us reading this book think of that more often hangs its women out to dry? I felt a nagging frustration to attempt this book, because this issue has been working on my nerves for quite some time: Why have our African American men been constantly backsliding more and more negatively for more than two generations? That would be from the end of the sixties until this time, which is 2013.

The most disappointing aspect is that this backward trend began to come about after President Lyndon B. Johnson, a Deep

South Democrat from Texas, did so much to help turn things around for black people.

Let me give you a little history. Lyndon B. Johnson (LBJ) was elected as the vice president during the presidential bid of President John F. Kennedy (JFK) in 1960. Many of us were doubtful about how well this presidency might work out for us. As fate would have it, John F. Kennedy was assassinated in Dallas, Texas, the home state of the vice president, on a campaign trip in November of 1963—Kennedy's final year of his only term in office. The rest is history.

Lyndon B. Johnson was sworn in as president, and in that swearing in, he promised to do the best he could to carry on the dreams that President Kennedy had already spoken to him about. Many of us were surprised that this Dixiecrat Democrat would be true to his word and attempt to do whatever he could for black people. But he fought for and got the Civil Rights Act passed. In the next year, he fought for and got the Voting Act passed. These were great victories for black people. One of them ended the Jim Crow laws that had been holding us back and that the federal government had ignored. The doors opened more than they had years before in 1954, when *Brown v. the Board of Education* became a mammoth win for us in education equality. And in President Johnson's last year in office, he had plans to launch what he had termed "the Great Society." But he decided not to run for reelection, as he was depressed and disconsolate with the way the Vietnam War was going.

Be that as it was, Mr. Johnson had taken us over two giant steps in helping to guarantee black people's rights and allow black people to believe we could successfully claim some of the rights that were part of the Thirteenth, Fourteenth, Fifteenth, and Sixteenth Amendments to the Constitution. In short, these actions and passages had allowed and enabled African Americans to vote, to have integration, and to have access to other previously denied rights.

These successful actions and passages under President Johnson caused the Dixiecrat Democrats to become so angry with what President Johnson had achieved to help black people that they decided en masse to bolt from the Democratic Party. They decided to join the Republican Party to show their disgust. For those who are still alive, you can still find them in the Republican Party today. These mean-spirited racists are, as I write these words, angry that a black man by the name of Obama ascended to the lofty heights of becoming the president of the United States.

This is a bit of important history, but we do not want to get too far off track from the actions and reactions of black men after the victories of 1954, 1965, and 1966. This backslide was disappointing after such important doors had been opened to African Americans. To not see the difference—the slide backward instead of a climb upward—one would have to have just arrived from another planet or awakened from a coma. I do want to make the point that this backslide does not refer to all African American males, but it does apply to most. My problem, as always, is that society judges and labels African Americans by what the worst of us do rather than by what the best of us achieve.

When I decided I was going to undertake this project, I feared I would be preaching to the choir and not to those who need to read this most. One reason is that many of the non-achievers and underachievers cannot read. Too many of them do not take kindly to reading, as that is "too white." For the same reasons that they do not like to read, they have no desire to acquire an education. I think I would be close if I made an educated guess that 90 percent of the group in question have never read any book from the first page to the last page. With that kind of attitude, how do they ever hope to really know about anything in any kind of factual way, if they never read or learn how to read? But let us not forget that these are the same people who will quickly complain and give lame excuses about why they are not able to achieve anything; they will claim racism is holding them back.

I need to make it clear that when I mention our African American young men, I am speaking of a group from ages fifteen to forty. It is hard to count those who are under fifteen, because one would think they could still have proper parenting and be saved. However, there are some cases in which even those who are under fifteen have gone astray, taken to the streets, and abandoned school. Those are the ones the parents have lost all control over. Those young men are totally lost, as they cannot be expected to enter the work market or take care of themselves or anyone else. Children who are living with single mothers and do not have any kind of significant male in the home, or out of the home, will more than likely be part of the forever-lost group. They will be forever ignorant, poor, and in and out of jail, and they might experience early deaths. This all comes about because they listen to the wrong people. When they listen to the wrong people, they come to the fork in the road around age fourteen, and they decide to take the wrong way. For whatever reason, they never learn anything about rules and discipline before they reach school age. Most of them also go off to school without the foggiest idea where they are going and for what purpose. We can chalk that up to poor parenting or missing parents. Some of those missing parents were right there in the home with them. They were what one would call negligent and missing in action.

We have now reached a time when these young black rappers are caught in a trick bag because they see ways to make unconscionable sums of money and ways to absolve themselves from any sense of moral responsibility. This was a statement made by Harry Belafonte. Spike Lee made the same point when he made a film about black advertising executives making money by selling depraved images of black people. The movie was called *Bamboozled*. *Bamboozled* means you are confused and lost, used and abused, while you think you are using the other guy. Dave Chappelle must be given credit for turning down a $50 million contract to put on a minstrel show, including skits featuring Rick James referring to women in a disrespectful way. At a subsequent taping in 2004, Chappelle was doing a skit in black face about a magical black pixie that tries to convince black people to play out the worst stereotypes, when a white man laughed out loud, and Chappelle stopped the taping. Chappelle realized that instead of using, he was being used. He realized that this was the sad reality of hip-hop and much of Chappelle's own comedy. Chappelle eventually walked away from the $50 million deal. He gave no official reason, but it seems that his conscience could not take it anymore. The sad fact remains that those who are still being minstrels don't really care. They have been bought out as clowns, saying, "Who cares what we look like as a race?" For example, some young black males walk around calling each other names that should be offensive to African Americans. But many African Americans have no concern or disgust at seeing such derogatory language used with each other—and out loud for everyone to hear. It appears as if we do not have any respect for ourselves and think we are doing something cute.

Too many of us also want to play the blame game for the crimes that black men commit. We do not want to take any personal responsibility for the failures or the eventual criminal actions or the inactions of parents who let their children get to that point. Many of our parents see their young sons heading for a career in crime. They realize that they have waited too long to try to turn things around and just let the young males get further into a worse situation.

On Sunday mornings on MSNBC, there is an early show called *Up with Steve Korncaki*. It is a show with a panel of guests talking about various subjects. On a show on June 2, 2013, a black female panel member brought up the subject of black male unemployment. She quoted an unemployment rate of 13 percent and commented on how high that was. She went on to mention some reasons for the high rate for black men. But she never mentioned the fact that black young men also have the highest rate of dropping out of high school. She ignored the fact that people do not hire black young men, or not-so-young men, and pay them money, when those men lack the skills and competence to perform the jobs that the employers are going to pay them for. This is just another instance in which we need to stop calling everything racism, when we fully realize we have shot ourselves in the foot.

Black rappers also do their part in helping to reinforce the idea of a black man as an unemployable, stupid oaf. In the words of Stanley Crouch, formerly of the *Village Voice*, young black men are thugs who are "monkey-moving, gold-chain-wearing, illiteracy-spouting, sullen, combative buffoons." Who would hire such a person? Who would want to live next to them? Who would want to help them? The statement goes on to say this is a twenty-first century version of D. W. Griffith's *Birth of A Nation*, the 1915 film that demonized former slaves as rapists, murderers, and thieves while glorifying the Ku Klux Klan.

But I'm sad to say that this notion seems to reflect black young men as a majority today. This is where too many not-so-young black men also are. They have managed to stay alive but live lives with no redeemable meaning. This issue is something that black leaders, black ministers, and black citizens in general need to discuss more. These young men are born, go to school for a few years in lower grades, achieve little academically, and move on into the teen years and drop out of school. Their next move is onto the streets, where the gang recruiters are waiting for them. They are naive and think they are doing something great by joining up with a group that will help them accelerate their life into a lot of negativity, nothingness, prison, and possible violent death.

The ultimate question becomes this: How can these young black men be so stupid today that they would opt for such emptiness and nothingness instead of opting for lives full of positives and the possibility of being successful, learned, and respectful citizens?

Chapter 6 Inspirational Choice

The Achievement of Frederick Douglass

For African Americans to know what we have had to endure in this country, we have to know what Frederick Douglass had to go through in his attempts to help us reach some kind of freedom and respect in this country. He was an activist, an abolitionist, an orator, and one of the strongest persons who ever tried to deal with our race and the slavery problem. This man was born in slavery, but never in his lifetime did he allow the problems he faced to keep him from becoming a person who would rise to be one of the greatest African Americans of all times.

Frederick Douglass was born in Tuckahoe, Maryland, in 1818. At birth, he was given the name of Frederick Augustus Washington Bailey. He was born to a slave mother, as the Civil War was still forty-three years away when he was born. His mother's name was Harriett Bailey. As was the case during the years of slavery, his father was an unidentified white man. Early on, young Frederick was raised in the cabin of his maternal grandparents during the first few years of his life. His mother was only able to slip away at night infrequently to see him and visit with him.

Frederick's first bondage experiences came when he was six years old and was brought to a nearby wheat plantation owned by Colonel Edward Lloyd. Frederick remained there for two years and then was sent to Baltimore to become a laborer in the household of Hugh and Sophia Auld. There he remained until he was fifteen years old.

It was against the law for slaves to learn to read and write at the time, but Frederick secretly taught himself to read and write by studying discarded newspapers. The most important thing he learned was that there were national debates going on regarding the pros and cons of the value or the evil of slavery. He also began to attend free black churches. In the churches, he was impressed and gratified when he saw free black men reading and speaking out publicly in the preferred style and rhetoric of the time.

Sometime later, Thomas Auld, the son of Hugh and Sophia, took Frederick to another plantation. This place was near the town of St. Michael, Maryland. Soon after his arrival there, Douglas organized a secret school for slaves. A mob of local whites soon discovered and broke up the school. To try to discipline Frederick, Thomas Auld hired him out to another local farmer who had a wide reputation as a slave breaker. Be that as it was, Frederick continued to become more and more defiant. He became so defiant that he refused to allow himself to be whipped. The Aulds again decided to hire him out at another plantation to another local farmer. When this happened, he put together another secret school for slaves. In their sessions, Frederick and his pupils began to discuss and devise plans of escape to the free state of Pennsylvania or some other free state in the north. But again, his school was discovered, and they could not put their plans into action.

By now, his owner, Hugh Auld, realized that Frederick was always going to be a constant problem. Realizing this, in 1836, he returned Frederick to Baltimore and hired him out to a shipyard where he learned how to be a caulker. Being on this job and being in the city of Baltimore, Frederick found himself having some relative freedom, and he was able to join a self-improvement society of black caulkers. This was yet another group where he heard debates on the major social and intellectual questions and issues of the time.

For some time, Frederick had been thinking about the idea of making some kind of proposal to the Aulds to buy his freedom. He made the proposal, but they turned him down. In September of 1836, he managed to escape by dressing as a sailor, wearing the clothing of a free black man of Baltimore, and carrying the papers he had as a seaman. This ruse enabled him to travel by train and steamboat and make it to New York.

Once in New York, he married a domestic maid by the name of Anna Murray. She was also from Baltimore and had earlier encouraged Frederick to go through with his escape plans. After he escaped, he changed his last name from Bailey to Douglass so that he would have a better chance of eluding potential captors and not getting returned to Baltimore. He was also able to use the experience he had gained as a caulker to land a job as a caulker and outfitter on whaling ships.

Frederick and Anna had two daughters and three sons over a ten-year period. They eventually moved to New Bedford, Massachusetts. There he joined the local African Methodist Episcopal Zion (AME Zion) church. With the practice he'd had earlier, he immediately became an active lay leader, speaker, and exhorter for black causes.

In New Bedford, Frederick was drawn more and more into the anti-slavery movement and began to attend regular meetings of the Massachusetts Anti-Slavery Society on Nantucket Island. It was there that he met and became friends with William Lloyd Garrison, an ardent abolitionist and editor of *The Liberator*, the leading abolitionist journal of the era.

During the next two years, Frederick and his family moved on to Lyon, Massachusetts. His fame continued to spread, and he made hundreds of anti-slavery speeches in northern New York, Ohio, Indiana, and western Pennsylvania. By 1843, Frederick had joined other leading abolitionist speakers on the 100 Convention Tour. He started to not only speak out against slavery but also do sensible, critical analysis regarding Northern racial prejudice. This led others to give him advice, saying that he might need to talk in simple terms, be a bit more halting in the way he spoke, and return to the way he'd spoken earlier in his anti-slavery advocacy. He was told that he might need to put a "little more of the plantation" in his speeches. However, by this time, Frederick did not want this kind of advice. During the years of 1844 and 1845, he was able to write the story of his life. He called his book *Narrative of the Life of Frederick Douglass*, published in 1845. This forty-four-page book sold over thirty thousand copies in the United States and Britain. Within five years, the book had been translated into

French, German, and Dutch. As a result of his book's success, Frederick Douglass was catapulted into the position of the most famous black person in the world.

The downside was that his popularity moved him to a point where his liberty was threatened. His anti-slavery colleagues advised him to go abroad to Britain so that he could evade the would-be slave captures. Frederick took the advice and went to Britain, where he joined with Britain's abolitionists in denouncing the slavery in America.

His anti-slavery friends also helped him raise enough money to buy his freedom from the Aulds in 1847. He returned from Britain and moved again. This time, he moved to Rochester, New York. In Rochester, he launched his reform journal on a weekly basis. It was called the *North Star*. In 1851, he also started another publication called the *Liberty Party Paper*. He eventually merged the two publications since both openly endorsed political abolitionism.

By the time Abraham Lincoln became president, Frederick was able to speak with him and let him know that he was with him and the Republican Party all the way. The Republican Party of Lincoln had a moderate, anti-slavery platform. He spoke to Lincoln and convinced him to allow black men to fight in the Civil War with the Union, or the North. This was a deal that became real around 1863. By fighting in the Civil War with the North, because of their service, these black soldiers could buy their freedom from slavery. In the meantime, Frederick continued to speak out on the fact that this was the war to end slavery.

He continued to speak out after the Emancipation Proclamation and on into the Reconstruction period. Frederick never abandoned his fight for African American rights. It was reported that less than a month before Frederick's death in 1895, a young black man solicited his advice for an African American just starting out in the world. His advice, without hesitation, was "Agitate, agitate, agitate!" Another memorable quote from Frederick Douglass was "Learn a trade or starve!"

Frederick Douglass was a black man who dedicated his entire life to the freedom and improvement of black people.

The surest way to work up a crusade in favor of some good cause is to promise people they will have a chance of maltreating someone.

—Aldous Huxley

CHAPTER 7

The Great Stop-and-Frisk Debate in New York City

This chapter has to do with an ongoing debate that has been getting more and more intense in New York City since the middle of 2012. I returned to the city after going to Georgia to bury an over-ninety-year-old relative. When I returned, it was the day after the weekend just before Independence Day. I looked at the *New York Daily News* and almost went into shock when I read that in four of New York's five boroughs, there had been shootings—some were murders. These boroughs were Brooklyn (Kings), Queens, the Bronx, and Manhattan. The only borough that was not involved was Staten Island (Richmond). I immediately knew that something was not right in that picture. What had gone wrong? I knew that Staten Island was predominately white. Not considering myself an idiot, I knew that a lot of this horrendous mayhem was black-on-black crime and murder. I am black, and for that reason, I wondered why I should not be concerned about this. Well, I was so concerned that I wrote a letter to several black leaders in this city, asking them what they could do. I asked them what their response to such slaughters of black people by other black people was. I also stated that I thought it was scandalous that there had been no statements of outrage from people who professed to love the people of our race.

So I am going to tell you now that I have no real respect for the black leaders of today. The reason is because they are in their positions as a business rather than to do something to help us as a people get ourselves out of the deep ditch we are in. These people have a base, and their base happens to be the people who are not doing what they could do to help themselves move more toward some kind of independence. They are content to have these people run to them and say they need help for all of their woes.

I ask you, as readers of this book, to tell me what the black leaders of today have really done to help black people move up educationally and financially, stay out of prison, do better by their children (mainly the black males), or educate young black females to not have babies whom they will have to raise alone, as the fathers couldn't care less about them and the children? Tell me, readers of this book. When was the last time you heard any black leaders seriously address the subjects I just mentioned? If you cannot readily come up with some answers, this means that your so-called black leaders are not doing a good job of leading.

———ονον———

Now maybe we can move on to the issue of "stop, question, and frisk." The black-on-black crime that occurred during that July 2012 weekend put the spark under my behind to write this book. I had been asking myself for some time, "What is it that we as black people en masse are doing that is more positive than negative?" The answer is nothing!

As I said before, our black leaders of today are not leading us anyplace uplifting. They use black people who are down and out for their base. Those people become their cheerleaders. But when the sun sets, where are these cheerleaders? They are in the same place they were when the sun came up.

I have always felt I had the ability to use common sense and do logical reasoning, and I knew immediately that all of the shootings that occurred had been in 98 percent to 100 percent black enclaves. That being true, I knew that the perpetrators and the victims were all likely black. It did not take long for my thinking to be proven accurate. The police caught most of these shooters within a day or two. The only one I have not heard about getting apprehended were those who killed some people with an AK-47 in a nice neighborhood in Queens, Laurelton/Springfield Gardens, which is a 100 percent black community. So the question now becomes this: Where should the police go to look for perpetrators? Should they go into Times Square? Should they go into the Eastside, just below Fifty-Ninth Street? Should they go into the Upper Westside above 168th Street in Manhattan? Or maybe they should do their stops on Wall Street and in the Financial District.

My point is that in such a situation, we begin to move into the argument of what racial profiling and criminal profiling are.

Let us give the black protesters and leaders their due. Yes, the constitutional and civil rights of those who are stopped and frisked are impinged upon. But the greatest question is this: Aren't the people of color who are being shot to death at epidemic rates being denied their civil right to live and not be shot to death? Come on, black leaders and upholders of civil rights—do you count, in your fight for civil rights, the efforts to keep black people from being shot to death by other black people? There was a black leader who came to New York and preached in a church in Flatbush (Brooklyn) while the residents of the area were pleading with the NYPD to do more to protect them. They were afraid of being killed when they came out of their homes. They were also letting the city know that when they safely got their children to school and came home, they felt they could not sit near the window, because they could be shot.

You hear from all of these people who have "bully pulpits," but black people are being killed, or their children or relatives are not being heard from. That is another reason I wanted to write this book. I want to be a voice for the young children who are already dead, for those who are wondering when their day of death will come, and for black people who are asking, "Can someone please speak out for us?"

Note that I have not given out any names when saying I do not have a lot of respect for our black leaders of today. I am not calling out any names, because all of you black people out there know who they are. You know they are in Chicago, New York, and the other large cities of this country.

I now need to let you have some of the bare facts at the center of this stop-and-frisk debate. As I said, you will get the bare facts; I will not be attempting to tweak any of them. If you do not take my word for it, you can always go on Google and get the same information.

Some Pertinent Numbers

1. In 1990, there were 2,245 murders in New York City. In 2012, the number was either 419 or 414, based upon the source giving the information.

2. In 1994, when Rudy Giuliani became mayor, the NYPD began using CompStat technology. Through this process, it became much easier and faster to gather helpful demographic information, ethnic information, information on the regularity of crimes committed, and other valuable information to be used in determining where more surveillance and manpower could be used to solve dangerous crimes.

3. Gunshot crimes and murders were greater than two thousand for so long that the citizens and the city officials, whether Republicans or Democrats, were ready to accept whatever anyone came up with that had a chance of getting better results.

4. After the tragedy on September 11, 2001, many beat policemen were reassigned so that they could be on guard for the prevention of other terrorist attacks. Approximately six thousand police were taken away from their regular tasks. This loss of manpower in many New York City communities did not help in reducing murders.

5. Nationwide in 2009, just counting teenagers alone, there were 2,439 shooting deaths.

6. At no time on record had there been fewer than five hundred shooting deaths in New York City before 2012. That being the case, much acclaim was given to Mayor Bloomberg and Police Commissioner Kelly for bringing this awful number down to just over four hundred.

The above facts were acceptable data and statistics for the mayor and the NYPD. The information that follows, at this point, contains arguments presented by those who would like to see the stop-and-frisk approach ended.

The anti-stop-and-frisk people say that there were over 650,000 stops in 2012. They contend that these stops were way too many for the end results. They do not mention that these were not all new stops. Some of these people were stopped two or three times. I say *people* because not every stop was a male. However, they want to make it clear that most of the stops were of young black males. Young black males were labeled as those between the ages of seventeen and thirty-seven. Not all of these stops were of young black males, but most were. The next-highest number of stops was of young Hispanic males. Too many or not, the results were that 768 illegal firearms were removed from the streets and from the possession of some would-be killers. The black leaders contend that the recovery of "only" 768 guns was not enough to justify the actions of the NYPD. Their argument became mainly one of the civil and constitutional rights of blacks being violated through this procedure. So racial profiling became the major argument against stops.

Early in 2013 a report came out stating that in 2012, young black males were responsible for 77 percent of shootings. Young Hispanic males were responsible for 19 percent. That left only 4 percent for Caucasians, Asians, and other groups. The NYPD's argument then escalated to "Whom do you think we should have been doing more surveillance on? Whom did you feel we should have been doing more stops on?"

Even with these clear facts and statistics, black leaders all the way to the NAACP stuck to their black-profiling stance. This moves us on to a class suit brought against the city and the NYPD by a black man named David Floyd. David Floyd was the lead plaintiff. David Floyd happened to be a young black man who had been stopped twice.[4] The black leadership felt they had the perfect person to be the leader in this class-action suit. But more importantly, the case was given to Judge Shira Scheindlin to hear. This judge is not to be confused with Judge Judy Scheindlin of TV fame. Judge Shira Scheindlin already had a reputation going back to 1994, when she'd had ongoing battles with the NYPD.

Some history for the Floyd case dates back to the case of *Terry v. Ohio* in 1968. This was a similar kind of case, and then Chief Justice Warren handed down the final decision in that case. Judge Warren of the Supreme Court stated that a stop was permissible only when a police officer observed some unusual conduct that led him or her to reasonably conclude in light of his or her experience that criminal activity might be afoot. In other words, an officer needed "reasonable suspicion." So the argument of those who are against the stop and frisk policy, and the argument of Judge Shira Scheindlin, was this: What is "reasonable suspicion," and how is it different from "inarticulate hunches and furtive movements"? Earlier, "stop, question, and frisk" incidents were sometimes known as Terry stops.

---

[4] David Floyd is a medical student.

William Bratton, a longtime top-brass police officer who was once the police commissioner of Boston, New York City, and Los Angeles, made a statement that he felt was germane to this debate about the stop-and-frisk approach. Mr. Bratton said that this is a basic tool of any police department trying to save lives and lower crime rates in the cities and precincts where they do their jobs. He went on to say that it is something that happens daily and is one of the most fundamental practices in policing. During Mr. Bratton's years as the New York City commissioner, he was widely credited from 1994 through 1996 as being a commissioner who changed the basic orientation of the NYPD to a stance of being proactive and trying to prevent crime rather than just responding to it.

———※———

At this time, there is a form known as the UF-250. The purpose of this form is to allow the stopping officer to check off all of the relevant boxes to explain why he or she stopped the suspect. Some of these boxes refer to things like suspicious behavior, suspicious bulges in clothing, refusal to comply with the officer's directives, and other "furtive movements," which have to have a written explanation.

Since there were so many stops in 2012, the UF-250s had to all be looked at separately. The NYPD was looking for what came out of the 2012 stops and the information that ended up on the UF-250s. After all was said and done, the findings showed that in 2012, 82 percent of the forms showed that these more than six hundred thousand stops were justifiable. Twelve percent were ambiguous, and 6 percent were deemed unjustifiable. But now we need to look at these statistics and remember that the number-one perpetrators were black. The number-two perpetrators were Hispanic.

Going by the last census figures taken for New York City, we find that the black population is 23 percent. I think we can make a sensible, commonsense, logical conclusion that if 23 percent of this city's population is black, and if roughly half of those are females, we have a serious problem.

Sixty-four percent of the murder victims and 71 percent of the shooting victims were young African Americans males. As I stated earlier, young African Americans are from seventeen to thirty-seven years in age. If you do your math, you will find that only 4 percent of New York's killers by firearms wind up being nonblack and non-Hispanic.

I think you need to hear some words spoken by Commissioner Kelly when he dared to go into the National Political Networks Headquarters, which is the base for Reverend Al Sharpton. Commissioner Kelly told the group, "We as a city, as a society, cannot just stand idly by in the face of these facts."

In spite of this visit, and in spite of the commissioner repeating the published facts for the attendees, the black leadership in the city of New York continued to stick by their stance of stop the "stop and frisk." It would seem to anyone with the ability to engage in logical reasoning would come to the conclusion that ending stop and frisk without presenting a thorough and detailed alternative is simply advocating a "no-plan" plan. Any alternative plan would have to successfully argue how such a plan would bring a greater measure of safety to these violence plagued communities vs. the reduction in violence achieved by the NYPD's stop and frisk tactic. The only thing that the black leadership had to say was that the stop-and-frisk method was racial profiling and was unconstitutional. They never stated a plan to help. The worst part was that they turned their backs on the other black people who were the innocent and victimized African American citizens. These African Americans were seeing their children and other family members or friends get shot and murdered by a host of young black men who were still under the age of eighteen. As I write this, I have not heard anything from the black leaders regarding a plan for these perpetrators. It is almost as if they are saying, "Go on with your bad selves. We have your back."

The worst part is what happened on August 12, 2013, just as I was about to complete this chapter. On August 12, 2013, Judge Shira Scheindlin gave her ruling against the city and the NYPD. That ruling maintained that the stops could only continue with a person to be named by the judge as an independent inspector. That person's job would be to decide if the stop was done properly or not. If it was not done properly, the person who was stopped would have the right to sue the City of New York. There was also a provision wherein certain chosen precincts would have to put cameras on their police persons to record the stops. This happened on August 12, 2013. On August 15, 2013, the city appealed this decision.

As I close this chapter, the only thing left to say is that the race for the new mayor of the city is nearing the voting day. The stop-and-frisk issue is big with the candidates. There are seven candidates—five Democrats and two Republicans. I bet you could decide how this is shaping up. All of the Democrats are against the stop-and-frisk practice. The two Republicans are already stating that they are with the mayor and the police commissioner, in favor of continuing the tactic. New York City is a Democrat city, and all of the Democratic candidates are betting that they will get the black vote if they are anti-stop-and-frisk. What they do not realize is that there are quite a few black people who are not in favor of getting rid of the stop-and-frisk tactic, particularly those living in the most dangerous areas; those who have already lost children, relatives, or friends to the rampant gun violence; and those who fear for their own lives.

The rationale for the city has been given in the statistics and released numbers that were published. On the other side, the anti-stop and frisk advocates have stated that they feel the stops are unfair, are unconstitutional, and violate the civil rights of too many young black men who should not be stopped. The city points to the large drop in shooting and killing incidents over the past year and a half as a reason to continue their stop tactic. The black leadership and other politicians say that the frisks cannot be credited for the large percentage of decreasing gun crime. Their argument is that crime is dropping in New York City and in other larger cities.

The only problem with the evidence the anti-stop and frisk people are giving is that they have no way to prove that the police tactic had nothing to do with the lower crime rate. Until more reliable evidence can be given, it is hard to believe that some miracle happened in which those doing the shooting for over a decade somehow had changes of heart and decided they wanted to become better citizens.

If this were true, it would be a great beginning to a better future for black people living in the most noted killing grounds in New York City, Chicago, Los Angeles, Philadelphia, Atlanta, Detroit, and other large American cities.

I am putting this chapter to bed this morning, which is August 24, 2013. However, I have to say that as I woke up this morning, the first thing I heard on the news was that a three-year-old black boy had been shot in the head in the Flatbush section of Brooklyn. He was taken to Kings County Hospital and is in critical condition. So we have a situation of who's "zooming" who that will only be decided after the shooting, killing, and murdering statistics for 2013 come out when the year is over. Until then, all I can say is what a pity!

Chapter 7 Inspirational Choice

Achievements of Paul Laurence Dunbar

Chapter 7 does not lend itself to any particular inspirational black leader, as it was a chapter that had pros and cons about blacks and pros and cons for the other side.

But Paul Laurence Dunbar is a great choice based on what he was able to accomplish. Mr. Dunbar was an African American poet born in 1872. He was a dialectic poet, meaning that he wrote his poems in the way black people spoke during his childhood. He was born just after the end of the Civil War. It is good for us to realize what so many of our black forerunners were able to achieve long before we appeared.

Paul Lawrence Dunbar was a child of slaves and was born in Dayton, Ohio. The period of his childhood was the Reconstruction. Both of his parents had been slaves on a plantation in Kentucky. He would listen to his parents as they told stories about the way life was when they were slaves. These stories became the basic foundation for his folk poetry.

Mr. Dunbar was able to attend Dayton, Ohio, public schools and had the notoriety of being the only student of color to attend Dayton High School. And more important, he became the class president. He also became the editor of the school paper, the president of the literary society, and the class poet. This was truly amazing for a student who was the only African American in the school.

After graduating from Dayton High School in 1891, he chose to pursue a career in journalism. At first, he found it difficult to nail down a writing job, mainly because of his race. During those in-between times, he took a job as an elevator operator and was known as "the Boy Poet."

Later on, continuing to pursue his dream, he was able to take out a loan to use in publishing his first book of poetry. The name of that book was *Oak and Ivy*, published in 1893. Later, in 1893, he was given the opportunity to read his poetry at the

World Columbian Exposition in Chicago, Illinois. At that time, Frederick Douglass and other prominent African Americans took note of him and offered great praise of his prominence as a poet.

He moved on to publish his second book, which was entitled *Majors and Minors*, published in 1895. A well-known critic by the name of William Dean Howells noticed this second book. He was responsible for having *Majors and Minors* redone and expanded into a new version with the title *Lyrics of a Lovely Life*, published in 1896. The mainstream publisher of the day, Dodd and Mead, did the publication, and Dunbar became famous among black and white audiences. Not long afterward, his fame and reputation spread overseas.

Though his use of dialect alienated some of the later African American readers, W. E. B. Dubois and Nikki Giovanni, who came along long after Paul Laurence Dunbar, praised his work. The two aforementioned recognized the challenges Paul Lawrence Dunbar faced at the turn of the century as a black poet. They recognized that what he was doing at the time was attempting to sound a "deeper note." William Dean Howells was also important to his success, as an early critic.

As fate would have it, Paul Dunbar passed away as a relatively young person in 1906, at the age of thirty-three. Three years before his death, he penned a poem that has been praised as one of his most important, "The Poet," which was not done in dialect.

Paul Dunbar received the highest possible accolade when the first black public high school in America was named Paul Laurence Dunbar High School in Washington, DC, in 1915. Many of the most famous black people were graduates of this high school.

Man is that creature who must have some criterion of the good ...

This means that the true realist is the man who acknowledges the distinction between good and evil.

—Edmond La B. Cherbonnier

The Phenomenon of Black Street Gangs: Who Are They, and What Are They?

Because of the havoc that the existence of black street gangs has brought over the past several years, especially in the realm of black-on-black violence, no book can purport to be an open letter to African Americans without addressing the issue of black street gangs. This discussion is now a necessity because these black gangs are not just an entity in the known black enclaves of our big American cities. These gangs are now a reality in our smaller cities, where, at one time, we never thought they would be an issue in need of discussion.

But in the year 2013, at the time I am penning this information, gangs are now a big issue that we as black people need to be concerned about. I heard that around mid-August 2013, the city of Trenton, New Jersey, had already passed the all-time record for the number of shooting deaths in any one year. That tells us that this issue is escalating.

The first thing I will attempt to do is trace the existence of street gangs back to where they began. I will then give some history regarding the first gang members and why they started this phenomenon. Then I want to try to trace, by dates or times, when blacks got started and how they got started.

My research shows that the earliest gangs in big urban areas got their beginnings in the city of Chicago, Illinois. Most of us do not realize that street gangs in Chicago go all the way back to the turn of the twentieth century. However, those gangs were not black. This chapter attempts to give a historical outline of how other street gangs led to the formation of black street gangs. Out of necessity, the information has to be much briefer than I would like it to be. However, if you would like to know more, I recommend you read a book called *Black Gangsters of Chicago*, by Ron Chepesiuk.[5]

Earlier nonblack gangs were comprised of many of the early white immigrants who had made their way to Chicago. These earlier gangs were called "gang boys," as they were primarily young male children of the immigrants. They were living in a new big city's industrial slums. It is important to remember for us as African Americans that this was where gangs began— in the industrial slums of this big urban American city. Their formation was a natural response to the problems and contradictions of their new world. Their mode was an adaption that included rituals, symbolism, folklore, and concepts that provided a basis for solidarity and a sense of collective purpose. I ask you to please remember the above purpose of the white immigrants as we go further in this chapter.

It is good to know, as African Americans, how important Chicago is and was to this country and to us as African Americans. We might be surprised that we can trace the beginning of gangs to Chicago as early as 1850. Think about it—this time was more than a decade prior to the American Civil War. By that time, Chicago had reached the status of third-largest city in the United States, and it already had a

---

[5] Ron Chepesiuk, *Black Gangsters of Chicago* (Fort Lee, NJ: Barricade Books, 2007).

population that was largely foreign born. These foreigners were from England, Ireland, Germany, and Italy. By 1890, 80 percent of Chicago was foreign born. This came about due to the addition of Greeks, Bulgarians, and Polish immigrants.

With these diverse populations, cultures, and religious leanings, it is reported that there were more than one hundred languages spoken in Chicago. However, Chicago also has black fame. First of all, as I am writing this in September 2013, Chicago remains the American city with the second-largest black population of any other American city in the country.

It is important for us, as African Americans, to know that the first permanent resident of Chicago was a black Haitian named Jean Baptiste Point du Sable. Mr. du Sable was a Haitian trader who was of African-French descent. In the year 1779, du Sable built Chicago's first permanent settlement, near the mouth of the Chicago River. It was a trading post with nine buildings, which included businesses.

Jean Baptiste Point du Sable's accomplishments happened eighty-one years prior to the beginning of the Civil War in 1861. This black enclave, through the 1840s and 1850s, was a major terminus for the Underground Railroad, which thousands of escaped slaves passed through on their way to freedom.

As the years passed, many other blacks heard about Chicago and found it a good place to migrate to. Most of those blacks found their way into Chicago's Southside by 1910. These migrations helped Chicago to grow a black population of over forty thousand. As more and more blacks came into Chicago, obvious race problems smoldered.

During the years between 1890 and 1960, vice in the black communities of Chicago was no well-kept secret. For instance, a black woman by the name of Vin Fields had the distinction of starting the largest house of prostitution in the country. Her prostitution population was said to have reached as many as seventy women under her madam-ship. Her house was also notable for having all black women who only had white men as clientele. Other than prostitution, there was also widespread gambling managed by blacks, including dice games, poker with chips, and card games, all on a regular basis. However, over time, the most lucrative gambling game became "policy playing," commonly known as playing the numbers. The name that comes up most often as the black policy king is John "Mush Mouth" Johnson. "Mush Mouth" took over the policy game from a man who was previously the main figure, Sam "Policy Sam" Young. Young had immigrated to Chicago from Huntsville, Alabama.

We can see from this brief history that big trouble would be arriving in Chicago once the era of the black street gangs began with seriousness. Gangs of white immigrants from many different European nations had already formed to protect themselves from each other. With the swelling of the black population in Chicago, it did not take much intelligence to understand that there would be run-ins between the blacks and the whites. Unnamed barriers and borders were understood to be places where blacks were not to tread. Some of these borders were as large as certain parkways. Certain streets defined other boundaries. Gangs of black or white color have always staked out territory that they vigilantly protect.

In Chicago, the violence between black gangs and white gangs reached an all-time peak on July 27, 1919. This was a ninety-six-degree day, and many people were looking for ways to escape the heat. A young black boy by the name of Eugene Williams went to the beach. He inadvertently swam south of Twenty-Ninth Street and entered an area of the water that had White Only signs all around. The whites became so infuriated that they began to throw stones at him. A stone hit Williams in the forehead and knocked him unconscious. He went underwater and drowned. A friend of his tried unsuccessfully to save him, but the aftermath was the beginning of the 1919 Chicago Riot. Some writers dubbed the days of rioting as the Chicago Red Summer of 1919.

By the 1960s, many black street gangs had formed, and many of them were taken over by other larger, more-populated, stronger black gangs. Some of the most well known, or notable, were the Vice Lords and the Blackstone Rangers. For a brief period prior to the assassination of Dr. Martin L. King, the two above-mentioned gangs were looked upon with some measure of respectability. Dr. King rented an apartment in Chicago in the territory of the Vice Lords. They let him know that they were volunteering to look out for him in the way of security. They began to receive funds from sources as well lauded as the Ford Foundation. They used some of these charitable funds to do things for community children. There were outings and other affairs. However, there were many who saw these activities as just cunning methods to recruit young men into their gang.

All of the good work they were supposedly doing ended when Dr. King was killed in 1968. Then the serious vying with the Blackstone Rangers began, leading to a serious competition to see who would be able to absorb the smaller gangs into their operation. The area of protection for the Rangers was Woodlawn. The Vice Lords' territory, or area of protection, was Lawndale. Like many of the gangs of today, they moved quickly from fights with blunt instruments and knives to handguns.

Era of the Latter-Day Black Street Gangs

So far, I have focused the narrative of black street gangs on the gangs of Chicago. That was necessary because Chicago had the earliest black street gangs, and they have, over the years, had the most black street gangs. Anyone who pays any attention to the news will have no problem realizing that Chicago's gangs continue to wreak an enormous amount of violent havoc. The book *Black Gangsters of Chicago* contains three hundred pages of information on Chicago's black street gangs. I thank Mr. Chepesiuk for his book. It has been most valuable to me in penning this chapter.

We can now look at the two gangs that are arguably the most well known and have received most of the press coverage: the Cripps and the Bloods. Available information has declared that the Cripps formed before the Bloods but not too much earlier. The Cripps were born as a street organization in 1968, founded by Raymond Lee Washington in the south-central area of Los Angeles, California. According to the local folklore, their name was formed from a combination of *crib* and the acronym *RIP* (meaning "rest in peace"). This name denotes the intergenerational nature of the gang membership from birth to death. Other important Cripps include Stanley Tookie Williams, a founder of the West Side Cripps, and his two right-hand men. They were Michael Concepcion and Jamel Barnes. It is also important to mention that the FBI and other law-enforcement agencies have described the Cripps as the largest, most violent, most notorious gang in the history of the United States. There are reports that this gang has spread, in smaller or larger form, to most cities in the United States. And at this time, there is information suggesting that the Cripps are emerging in many suburban areas in the United States and around the world.

The Bloods emerged as a street gang as a direct result of conflict with the Cripps. Rumor has it that the Cripps initiated the conflict in the early 1970s. It seems as if Los Angeles black street gangs have a tradition of creating set alliances for fighting common enemies. The Cripps began in the late 1960s and early 1970s to launch aggressive campaign strategies to absorb some gangs and bring the rest into submission. This aggressive strategy prompted a diverse group of sets to join and form the Bloods in order to confront the Cripps.

These are the names of some of the other groups that the Bloods were able to get to join them in their conflicts with the Cripps: the Slausons, the Huns, the Farmers, the Gladiators, the Businessmen, and the Pueblos. They were also late-1960s gangs in Los Angeles, known more commonly as the Hustlers. These Hustlers had formerly been a bond between some other groups, such as the Pirus, the Brims, and the Bishops. They were groups that were counting on surviving their precarious social and economic environment by getting together to make money by running numbers, or selling drugs (e.g., marijuana, cocaine, acid, whites, and blues). They also took advantage of naive youth.

These early Hustler groups already had a history of getting into frequent fights with white groups, but rarely did they use extreme violence to win their fights or achieve their goals. Their violence and fights were limited to fist fights and the use of belts and knives. Another unusual thing about the Hustlers was that they wore slick, stylish zoot suits; Stacey Adams shoes; nice slacks; straps; and brim hats. In other words, their stylish clothing identified their group(s). The Brims actually took their name from the brim hats they wore. When I first read about them, I liked the idea that they had some style and did not decide to have the thug look.

As I said earlier, the Cripps had a campaign geared toward smaller-group absorption, as was the case with the Hustlers and cliques made up of other youth groups. It was this passion of the Cripps that placed in motion the Hustler group's alliances. They then transformed into bangers that resulted in the creation of the Bloods.

In 1971, the Pirus became a strong enough set from Compton to declare wars against the Westside Cripps. These wars were originally fistfights that occurred at local high schools and Leaders Park. Not long after, the Cripps and the Pirus started to use guns to settle their conflicts. In a period of three years, the fights between the Pirus and the Cripps gained national attention. One Pirus leader reported that ten of their members had been killed. When an original leader of the Pirus, Lyle Joseph Thomas, a.k.a. the Bartender, was killed by the Westside Cripps, a big decision was reached: because of the killing of Thomas, the Pirus and the Brims decided to join as a unit with the Bloods.

The Pirus and the Brims also decided they would begin to use the red bandana as their signature item of identity. The term *blood* had long been a part of the lexicon of southern blacks. It was a greeting, as in, "Hey, blood." They likened it to greeting a family member. This term caught on, and the Blood Alliance formed, along with the red flag group signature that the Brims had first used.

—*ᖇ*—

Street Gang Structures

Both the Cripps and the Bloods began as loose networks of small gangs structured as federations of independent gangs. Blood members rarely use the term *gang* to identify their groups. They prefer the use of the word *hood*, which can also identify their geographical area(s). Any set might, at one time or another, agree to shift alliances with other Blood sets to wage war against the Cripps. Bloods also have no written constitution, formal norms, or rules and regulations. They become members and learn their code of conduct by interacting with other seasoned members who will teach them orally what it means to be a Blood. However, there is one basic tenet that all members learn immediately: they are bound by a code of silence.

The Cripps' organizational structure lacks codified rules and regulations. They operate in a flexible and malleable manner. Their sets create alliances with one another mostly in order to fight archenemies, such as Chicano and Latino gangs of the area. Sometimes their looseness has worked against them, when some of their most violent fights have broken out as Cripps-to-Cripps rivalries. An example of this would be the Eight Trays versus the Rolling 60s.

The Cripps' origin contains three main narratives to explain their existence. The first is the narrative that places this gang in the context of institutional racial violence encountered by southern blacks moving into the city of Los Angeles. The second narrative is one that places the origin of the Cripps within a political context and explains its emergence as a product of the political vacuum created by the undermining of political community-based organizations, such as the Black Panthers and the United Slaves. Their third narrative is what can simply be described as a group of hoodlums and drug dealers who came together to victimize their own communities.

Over the years, there have been some efforts to get the Cripps to be more positive. Ex–Black Panther member Mumia Abu-Jamal traces the origins of the Cripps to a community-based organization named Community Relations for an Independent People—to spell the acronym CRIP. They attempted to espouse the ideas of self-determination, black nationalism, and activities in the community that included cultural affirmation and socialization. However, the Cripps were developing in an era when the black community was experiencing extreme social, political, and economic marginalization. So instead of going in the direction of positivity, they instead went in the direction of war against the political and community goals and became lost in a vicious circle of endless violence for street supremacy.

As I explained earlier, this was when the emergence of the Bloods' strength began. In the early 1970s, the Cripps' recruiting efforts were ruthless.

Summary of the Black Street Gangs

In this chapter, I have attempted to explain the history of street gangs, some of the most known locations, names of some of the leaders or founders, and some information on their group activities. At this point, I will give a summary of just what they are and what they stand for.

The typical street gang develops in opposition to mainstream (middle-class) values and institutional sources of judgment. Their subculture mentality is based in shocking outsiders, asserting distaste, and showing distaste for dignity. They are mainly youthful males whose habits and values are incongruent with the institutional logic of middle-class society. This incongruence leads them into trouble when these young men purposely act out in overly masculine and confrontational ways.

These groups are social and criminal subcultures. *Subculture* refers to something that is against whatever society considers normal. The gangster mentality tells you that you should be in conflict with the ways in which normal people behave. Once in a gang, you have taken an oath that says you are all about existing in criminal and violent activities.

The gang recruiters are experts at preying on the minds of young and naive black males. In the inner-cities, where there are housing projects, they watch young black males and know when the time is right for them to swoop down on them and welcome them into their gang. They begin to brainwash them with protection rhetoric. They then move on to getting these young black males to accept the mistruth that going to school is a waste of time. Their greatest selling point is to get them to believe they could be making money immediately without sitting in a classroom anymore, reading books and studying.

The real pity is that most of these youngsters have no significant positive male figures in their lives. They also find it hard to compete with the middle-class students and those who do have adult males as leadership role models. That disadvantaged youngster is one who can easily be persuaded to buy into the black street-gang lifestyle. Once he commits himself, he is automatically on a one-way street to a life of crime, prison time, or likely death at an early age.

To end this chapter, I have chosen to paraphrase a few words from a 1970 three-week number-one hit in the rhythm-and-blues field. The song was "War." It was a hit for a man named Edwin Starr. The question was "War—what is it good for?" The answer in the refrain was "Absolutely nothing!" And now I ask, "Black street gangs—what are they good for?" The answer is the same: "Absolutely nothing!"

Chapter 8 Inspirational Choice

Malcolm X/Malcolm Little

Malcolm X, or Malcolm Little, was the youngest person I chose as an inspirational choice for this book. He also had a storied past. Because of this storied past, I need to include a lot about his early years. This information will reveal an interesting picture of how he became the adult that he was.

Malcolm's father was a man by the name of Earl Little Sr. He was a man who was known to be an accomplished carpenter, a good brick mason, and a minister. These were qualities that made him a proud black man. He resided in a southwest-Georgia town called Reynolds. It is no surprise that Earl Sr. had run-ins with the whites of the small southern-Georgia town. His run-ins became too much for him to handle, and he made up his mind to leave Reynolds. His wife at that time was a woman named Daisy Mason. When he left, he was also leaving behind three children born from his marriage to Daisy. Those children were Ella, Mary, and Earl Jr.

Earl eventually made his way all the way to Canada, to the city of Montreal. There he met a light-complexioned woman by the name of Louise Langdon Norton. She too had made it to Montreal after leaving her home and native country of Grenada. The circumstances surrounding why and how she came to Canada are unknown. However, Earl got married to this woman, even though he had never gotten a legal divorce from Daisy.

Earl was a man who had activism in his blood in fighting for black causes. While in Montreal, he heard about a new black movement called UNIA (the United Negro Improvement Association). The founder of this movement was Marcus Garvey, who gained widespread popularity among black people around the year 1920. Garvey was a Jamaican who also widely spoke of the Back to Africa Movement. He made his major location Harlem in New York City. Garvey first came to New York

81

around 1918. When Earl Sr. heard about the Garvey movement, he could not wait to meet this man. In 1919, while still living in Montreal, Earl Sr. got to meet Garvey. He immediately joined UNIA and became one of its most serious spokesmen.

In 1921, at a Harlem gathering that six thousand black people attended, they declared UNIA an international black organization. Earl Sr. then became even more dedicated to UNIA's goals and aspirations. This information is necessary to know, because it speaks to where Malcolm Little received his activist grounding. It is also necessary to mention that Malcolm was still unborn at this time. He would be the fourth child born to Earl Sr. and Louise. His birthday was May 9, 1925. His place of birth was Omaha, Nebraska, at Omaha University Hospital. In the Midwest at that time, the Ku Klux Klan was just as active in Omaha; Lansing, Michigan; and Milwaukee, Wisconsin, as it was in the Deep South. Strangely enough, the KKK's presence coincided with the birth of UNIA and also with the time when Earl Sr. was full of zeal and fervor to do black activist work.

The next city that the Littles moved to was East Chicago, Indiana. By that time, the Klan had become even more vicious, creating a black-hating territory worse than some of the previous towns the Little family had tried to settle in. Adding fuel to the fire was the fact that Earl Sr.'s speaking engagements for UNIA had become more well known, which the racist whites disliked.

The Littles moved again, this time to a small house on the outskirts of Lansing, Michigan. The time of this move was in 1929. They had been there just a few months before trouble found Earl Sr. and his family again. They received a threat that they had to move. The reason the aggressor gave was that he had found a clause that forbade the sale of that property to any blacks. The threat further warned that their ownership had been voided.

On November 8, 1929, a large group of the hateful whites came in the middle of the night, doused the house with gasoline, and set it on fire while the family was sleeping. But for the grace of God and for the son, Wilfred, hearing the explosive boom as the fire started, the entire Little family would have perished on that November night. But they were able to escape with their lives.

At this time, Malcolm was just four years old. Memories of this kind of awful event helped turn him into the kind of adult with a mind-set that pushed him forward to the personality that America got to know. His travels with his father and the hatred his family faced caused him to begin to learn the violence-for-violence philosophy that became his trademark.

Malcolm the Adult

Malcolm Little, who became Malcolm X, had his mind made up to someday become a national leader in the fight for justice for black people. He was steadily getting his training from his father and the Garvey UNIA movement. Malcolm had already become a member of the Nation of Islam.

However, that was not his next step into adulthood. After his father's death, his mother found it difficult to carry on with the eight children she was left with. The great emotional and economic strain finally broke her. After someone found her walking in the snow and carrying a baby while barefoot, she was declared insane. The children became wards of the State of Michigan.

When he was a teenager, Malcolm's delinquent behavior landed him in a detention home in Mason, Michigan. When he became a bit older, he journeyed to Boston and then on to New York City. As a young adult, he acquired the name of Detroit Red. He got his skin tone and his reddish hair from his mother. In New York, Malcolm became involved in a life of crime. His crimes included number running, dope peddling, con games, thievery, and, eventually, armed robbery.

A few months before his twenty-first birthday, he was sentenced to prison in Massachusetts for the crime of burglary. During this period in his life, he became friends with another inmate, and his life was transformed enough for him to begin to appreciate the liberating value of education.

Through his family, he was able to discover the empowering religious and cultural message of Elijah Muhammad's Nation of Islam. The support of the family and the Nation of Islam, together, gave him what he had not had before: the self-respect he needed as a black person.

After spending almost seven years in prison, he was released in 1952. During this time in prison, he had honed his reading skills, his vocabulary, and his debating skills to a spectacular level. Stories have it that while incarcerated, Malcolm read on a daily basis.

Soon after Malcolm's release, Elijah Muhammad saw what a bright young man he had the fortune of having in his movement. Soon Malcolm was given the duty of minister in the Nation of Islam. His major themes were preaching against black self-hate and on behalf of black self-esteem. In June 1954, Elijah Muhammad appointed Malcolm as minister of Temple Number Seven in Harlem.

At first, Malcolm's messages were not popular with people in the African American community, as his philosophy was counter to the civil rights messages and tactics of Dr. Martin Luther King Jr. Malcolm was against nonviolence and also against integration. The media, both white and black, portrayed him as a person dedicated to violence and a teacher of hate.

Malcolm soon found that he could not continue to speak his own mind as long as he was a minister representing Elijah Muhammad and the Nation of Islam. Malcolm took his largest step out on his own by betraying his leader's authority when he said, in 1963, "The chickens are coming home to roost," in reference to the assassination of President John F. Kennedy in November of 1963. This remark by Malcolm X caused much envy, anger, and jealously in the Muhammad family circle. As a result of this rift, Malcolm soon after declared his independence and left the Nation of Islam. His departure was in March of

1964. His major goal was to further develop his own philosophy of the black struggle for freedom.

Malcolm went on to found the Organization of African American Unity (OAAU). By this time, he had begun to mock other black groups by calling them the "so-called Negro Revolution." He said that the civil rights movement was not a revolution. He mocked their goals and claimed they just wanted to integrate lunch counters, theaters, public parks, and public toilets.

His independence lasted for approximately one year before he was the victim of an assassination. During that short time, after he left the Nation of Islam and before his death, he made a pilgrimage to Mecca so that he could see the mainstream, original Muslims. From this journey, he began to transform his theology. He changed his name again, this time to El Hajj Malik El-Shabazz. He declared that orthodox Islam was incompatible with the racist teachings of Elijah Muhammad. Much of this came about from his travels in which he met white Muslims and other whites who were active participants in the liberation of African countries.

He hoped to use his organization of African unity as a platform for implementing his new ideas. But time ran out on February 21, 1965, when, as he was speaking, he was shot down by assassins at the Audubon Ballroom in upper Harlem.

Long after Malcolm's death, blacks in the African American community declared him one of the most famous liberators of black consciousness during the second half of the twentieth century. He was deemed a "cultural prophet of blackness." African Americans who are now proud of their blackness give much credit to the ideas of Malcolm X. Lastly, he is given much credit for helping black or African American studies to become mainstream subjects in colleges and universities.

The greatest magnifying glasses in the world are a man's own eyes when they look upon his own person.

—Alexander Pope

To err is human, but when the eraser wears out ahead of the pencil, you're overdoing it.

—J. Jenkins

CHAPTER **9**

The Evolution of Rap: A Brief Overview

Rap is a phenomenon that existed prior to when most people think it originated. A look into the *Webster New World Dictionary* gives the reader five definitions of *rap*. The first is to "knock or strike quickly." The next is to "talk seriously and frankly with another or others." We get to definition number five before we come to "a kind of music with rhymed verses chanted or declaimed to drums or synthesizers."

I could not find *gangster rap* in the dictionary, but the definition of *gangster* is stated as a member of a gang of criminals. These definitions are important to remember as you read on. Now I would like to move to definition number two, as it is germane to the subject of this chapter.

The Man Known as H. Rap Brown

The word *rap* first came into frequent and popular use in the black community, and also in the media, when H. Rap Brown came on the scene during the early 1960s. This young man in his twenties became a civil rights activist. His name at birth was Harold Gerald Brown, and he was born in Baton Rouge, Louisiana, in 1943. He started to refer to himself as H. Rap Brown when he gained notoriety after he assumed the chairmanship of one of the civil rights organizations. He took on the chairmanship of the Student Nonviolent Coordinating Committee (SNCC, pronounced as "Snick"). Under Brown, SNCC was seen as an ally of the Black Panther Party. One can readily see that this alliance could not last long, because the Black Panthers made no bones about the fact that they were not a nonviolent organization or group. The SNCC had the word *nonviolent* in its organization's name. There is no need to waste more time in explaining that H. Rap Brown only remained chairman of SNCC for about six months. He then moved on immediately to become the minister of justice for the Black Panthers.

H. Rap's fame grew as he made more and more volatile statements. One has to remember that when H. Rap was angrily speaking out, the Civil Rights Act was yet to be passed. The Voting Rights Act was yet to be passed, and just as importantly, Jim Crow laws were still in place. It is significant to mention that this era of H. Rap Brown was one when Malcolm X was still in prison in Massachusetts. It is important because we can see that H. Rap Brown was not copying anything from Malcolm X's playbook. At the time, Malcolm X was still Malcolm Little or Detroit Red. It is also significant to point out that when H. Rap was hurling volatile verbal bombs, Dr. Martin L. King Jr. was still alive.

Two of the statements that H. Rap became known for at the time still live on today. They got the attention of whites who hated us—and everybody else. One of those statements was "If America don't come around, we're gonna burn it down." The second statement was "Violence in America is as common as cherry pie." Both of these statements showed that H. Rap Brown was more of a Malcolm X–type thinker, before Malcolm X. He had rejected pacifist civil rights thinking and actions.

In the year 2000, H. Rap Brown was sentenced to life in prison for the murder of one of the two Fulton County, Georgia, sheriff deputies he shot. Only one of the two died, and because of that, H. Rap Brown will be in jail for life. He now goes by the name of Jamil Abdullah Al-Amin. As I write this in November 2013, H. Rap Brown is now seventy years old. He was no stranger to Huey Newton, Eldridge Cleaver, Stokley Carmichael, Angela Davis, or any of the other Black Panthers.

One last thing I need to say about H. Rap Brown is that nothing he did had anything to do with singing or making money by selling music. He was speaking out on the actions of inequality toward black people. His claim to fame was largely saying things that got attention and upset the status quo. We can see reasons to be thankful for H. Rap Brown's contribution to our race and also what kind of legacy he has now that years have gone by.

In 1969, H. Rap Brown wrote his autobiography, entitled *A Political Autobiography.*

The First Music Rappers

During my research and preparation for writing this chapter, I came across the following comment in "The Encyclopedia of Gangs" (Kontos and Brotherton / pg. 201) - "A history has been constructed that links rap music to the black community, deindustrialization, and the urban poor. It is generally agreed that rap emerged in the Bronx New York, in the 1970's with three DJ's bringing it into public consciousness." I kept having a problem with this statement. I finally remembered that I had heard of a group prior to the 1970s Bronx period. The name of that group was the Last Poets. I remembered them because I asked myself, "What in the world is this?" I must admit that no rap music has ever moved me. The reason is because after listening to what I perceived as real music, I could never relate to people talking, especially people who cannot sing and who say monotonous things over loud beats.

I had been listening to all of the changes that had come about in music, from blues to jazz to rhythm and blues to soul to hip-hop. But when this talking music, which I never felt was music, came upon the scene, I could not relate to it. At any rate, it is for that reason that the name of the Last Poets came back into my memory.

Sure enough, when I searched for information about them, I found it. My memory of them was accurate. The Last Poets was the name of several group of poets and musicians who gathered in the late sixties as part of the African American civil rights nationalist movement. Take note here that this is yet another reference to people who were tied to the civil rights movement. However, this time, they decided to turn their protest into lyrics with musical beats behind them.

The Last Poets took their name from a poem by an African named Keorapetse Kgositsile. He was from South Africa, and anyone with a sense of history knows how bad things were for blacks in South Africa during the sixties. The poet Kgositsile wrote his poem thinking that he was living in the last era of poetry before the white guns would take over. The last group of individuals to use the name was the trio of Felipe Luciano, Gylan Kain, and David Nelson.

However, as it turns out, another version of the group, led by Jalaludin Mansur Nuriddin (aka Alafia Pudim) and Umar Bin Hussan penetrated rap culture in a significant way. The Last Poets have been cited as one of the earliest influences on hip-hop music. In his Allmusic.com profile of The Last Poets (URL accessed 7/04/2014) music critic Jason Ankeny wrote - "With their politically charged rap, taut rhythms, and dedication to raising African American Consciousness, The Last Poets almost single-handedly laid the groundwork for the emergence of hip-hop." Also, the British music magazine *NME* cited Gil Scott-Heron, the Last Poets, and, later, DJ Gary Byrd, as influential artists who paved the way for many of the socially conscious black spokespersons and emcees who would emerge a decade later.

The original Last Poets were formed on May 19, 1968, the birthday of Malcolm X, who was born on May 19, 1925. The group formed at the Marcus Garvey Park, just below 125th Street in East Harlem, New York City. They were most renowned for their inclusion on the soundtrack of the 1977 film *Right On*. The remainder of the 1970s saw a decline in this group's popularity. But in the 1980s and beyond, they still found some renown with the continuous rise of hip-hop music. They even began to get more acclaim when they were referred to as the fathers or grandfathers of the new movement. They also did some collaborative work on an album with the rapper Common, with a song produced by Kanye West entitled "The Carver." They have also done some work with Wu Tang Clan and other politically affiliated hip-hop groups. They worked with Black Market Militia on a song called "The Final Call." Anything they have done lately has been as featured artists on more recent hip-hop artists' albums.

Hopefully, this information has been helpful in getting the history correct regarding the fact that rap did not start in the Bronx.

Bronx, New York, Rap

As I stated in the preceding pages, the Bronx group known as the Sugarhill Gang was not the first to perform or record rap. They recorded "Rapper's Delight" in 1979, and it was the most highly acclaimed rap record at the time. This group's home base was Englewood, New Jersey. "Rapper's Delight" was really a hip-hop single that became the first of its generation to become a top-forty hit. It was a song that used the track from "Good Times," which had already been a hit by the group Chic. This was also the beginning of sampling, a technique that rappers still use in which they borrow music from earlier songs as their foundation.

The Sugarhill Gang's members were Michael "Wonder Mike" Wright, Henry "Big Hank" Jackson, and Guy "Master Gee"

O'Brien. They were assembled as a group by Sylvia Robinson of rhythm and blues fame, who had a huge fifties hit called "Love Is Strange," performed as Mickey and Sylvia. The other person who helped assemble this group was Sylvia's husband, recording mogul Joe Robinson, who was also the founder of Sugar Hill Records, choosing that name from an Upper Manhattan West section commonly referred to as Sugar Hill.

After the great success of "Rapper's Delight," the Sugarhill Gang never again had a song go as high on the charts as their original hit. They did have a number of minor hits, such as "Apache," "Eighth Wonder," and "Showdown." Ten years after "Rapper's Delight," the group reminted the song on a children's hip-hop album called *Jump on It*. Their last record to achieve any real toehold was a song called "Lala Song." In later years, around 2009, they also used the name Original Sugar.

For the purpose of this book, it is important to make it clear that no groups mentioned so far were referred to as "gangsta rappers." The Sugarhill Gang ultimately had five studio albums, nine compilation albums, and fifteen singles.

Gangsta Rap

Even though a number of scholars have discussed gangster rap, there is still debate over when gangster rap began. Some believe it started in the late 1980s, and others believe it began in the early 1990s. However, there is a consensus that the first to perform this altered version of rap was Todd Shaw, known as "Too Short." He began his gangster-rap career in the early 1980s, when he started making and selling made-to-order mixed cassette tapes while still in high school.

Shaw sold his tapes for ten dollars each. They contained thirty minutes of some previously released music by other artists over which he would rap. He produced his first commercial project in 1985 and thus became the first gangster rapper. This was a project combined with NWA. NWA was credited with being the first gangster-rap group when they released their LP in 1986. Rapper Ice T produced a few singles in the early 1980s, but they did not achieve any real commercial success. Too Short partnered with a musician and producer called Shorty B, and this became the gangster rap that got enough success to start getting regular certification as platinum.

Too Short decided to move to Oakland, California. Once there, it was just a matter of time before he became a colleague of Tupac Shakur. Tupac is still remembered as the most commercially successful rap artist. Tupac reportedly had sales of over seventy-three million records worldwide. Todd "Too Short" Shaw was born in Los Angeles, California, in 1966. His mother, who was an active member of the Black Panther Party, reared him in the south-central community amid the upheaval of the civil rights movement and, importantly, the formation of the black-power paradigm. He listened to music on station KDAY, which was an Afrocentric station that broadcast black music and whose deejays were often viewed as political leaders of the community. It was a station where funk musicians stood as proof of the effectiveness of black power.

Too Short is not only a so-called dirty rapper who tells stories of sexual prowess but also a social rapper, as was his colleague and bandmate Tupac Shakur. Both of them told stories from an organic perspective. They also spoke of resistance to the dominant culture and openly spoke in favor of community cohesion, even at the level of the street gangs. The rap from Todd Shaw and Tupac Shakur preached that these gangs gave or provided more support than the oppressive society at large. The connection of street gangs to the Black Panther Party is well documented, and Too Short's mother was a member of the Los Angeles branch of the Black Panther Party. Bunchy Carter, a member of the Renegade Slauson gang, which would later become the Cripps, formed this branch.

Too Short moved to Oakland with his mother. Oakland, California, was the seat of the Black Panther Party. Too Short was just twelve years old when he went to Oakland, and he immersed himself early on in black-power ideology. Gangster rap became a common kind of expression in homes where parents were members of the Black Panther Party. As a group that supported black power, they hated all people who were racist toward black people. This would seem to be a group that was not so bad. Their point of view identified "the political economy as the superstructure which contributed to their lesser status as African-Americans, and also to the high levels of unemployment within their communities." ("Encyclopedia of Gangs" / Pg. 203). Their subsequent direction, however, seems to be misguided as "the men who were to become gangster rappers or rap artists, were not looking for gainful employment per se. Jobs were in the hands of the racist capitalist ruling class which forced them to react accordingly." ("Encyclopedia of Gangs" / Pg. 203).

Even though rap music is now popular, this music has not received a response in the United States that is favorable, especially gangster rap. "Rap is framed as dangerous to society. And protection of individuals (especially women and children) within society is invoked to combat the harm disseminating from this music."("Encyclopedia of Gangs" / Pg. 205). In 2006, the Parents Music Resource Center (PMRC) had a brief written by the ACLU "to wage a persistent campaign to limit the variety of cultural messages available to American youth by attacking the content of some of the music industry's products."

The PMRC has collective actions that include a demand for a warning label meant to alert consumers of themes within certain products deemed offensive, such as sexual messages, violence, drug or alcohol use, suicide, or the occult. Sanctions by the PMRC have also included prosecutions of record companies and store owners for distribution of nefarious material.

I found most of the above information in the "Encyclopedia of Gangs" - a book published in 2007. It would not be surprising to find much of the language used in gangster-rap records a lot worse than it was in 2007.

Gangster rappers are mostly a "cultural of me" and a "culture of disrespect." They are disrespectful to women, and they do not care if children hear the vulgar profanity they spew. It is surprising for me to see how many of our black young women do not find gangster-rap music revolting when the rappers speak of them in such filthy ways. One would think they would have more respect for themselves. Some rappers' messages are filled with the *N*-word, which shows that they have no respect for our race or for themselves. The "culture of me" comes from them not caring about anything as long as they can get money.

Lastly, we can see from this evolutionary overview of rap that rap, especially gangster rap, has a connection to street gangs and to crime. Most rappers take pride in having been in prison at one time or another. This criminal behavior gives them what they call "street cred." I feel I'm witnessing the demise of what had been black music for over five decades (blues, jazz, rhythm and blues, soul, pop-soul, and hip-hop), and this has been painful for me.

Chapter 9 Inspirational Choice

The Achievements of Langston Hughes

Langston Hughes was born in Joplin, Missouri, on February 1, 1902. His full name at birth was James Langston Mercer Hughes. His father was James Nathaniel Hughes but always preferred to be called Jim. His mother was Carrie Mercer. Jim, the father, was not only a proud and intelligent man but also a hardworking man. Jim had always had a problem with the lives of black people in the United States because of what he called "the color line." Before Langston was even a teenager, Jim took his money and went to live in Mexico. He made out quite well by purchasing a mine and a large parcel of land. He was eventually able to hire Mexicans.

After Jim left his son and wife, Carrie left Joplin and went to live with her mother, Mary Langston, in Topeka, Kansas. Langston's grandmother became a great influence on him, as she was always fond of him and his early intelligence. In 1915, Mary Langston died, and Langston's mother, Carrie, decided to move with Langston and her new husband to Cleveland, Ohio. It is worth noting that Langston, while living in Topeka, attended an all-white Topeka school, as there was no other school available for him to attend. Langston attended a white school in Topeka forty years prior to the *Brown v. the Board Of Education* case, which took place in 1954 and proved that white and black schools were separate but definitely not equal.

At Cleveland's Central High School, the talents and writing genius of Langston Hughes were immediately recognized. He wrote his first applauded poem at the age of fourteen. His talents were so recognizable and his English teacher, Ethel Weimer, was so impressed with him that she introduced him to the works of Carl Sandburg and Walt Whitman. Langston was impressed with the works of these two great American poetry icons and was able to learn quite a bit about his chosen field by capturing the unique style that they used.

Langston joined the staff of the *Central High Monthly* and became recognized by other already-well-known poets, such as Edgar Lee Masters, Edward Arlington Robinson, Amy Lowell, and Vachel Lindsay. On June 20, 1920, Langston and 126 other classmates marched down the aisle at Central High School. This would be the first of many important occasions that Langston Hughes would participate in.

Because of the decision by Jim, the father, to leave the United States, Langston had never had the opportunity to know him well or to develop any kind of meaningful relationship with him. Now that he was a high school graduate, Langston decided to take a trip to Mexico to do some bonding with his father. It seemed to be a good idea at the beginning. However, during that summer of 1920, when Langston talked about his decision to be a writer and poet, Jim was determined to talk him out of pursuing writing as an occupation. Instead, Jim wanted Langston to go to one of the well-known universities in Europe, study engineering, and return to Mexico and work with him as a head of his mine.

By the end of the summer in Toluca, Mexico, Langston was still set on pursuing a degree in journalism. Jim was not happy but told Langston he would pay for him to attend Columbia University for one year. Langston had applied for a scholarship from Columbia, but they never responded to him.

As fate would have it, Langston happened to come to New York City at the beginning of one of the most popular black eras in American history. He got caught up in what would become known as the Harlem Renaissance. This was a time that gave Harlem a rich legacy and is a time that is still remembered with pride. This 1920s movement saw some of the greatest artists in music, writing, and other art forms. Langston never returned to Columbia University after his one year there.

Although Langston only spent the one year at Columbia, he felt he'd been destined to come to New York and Harlem at the time that he did. Not only did he become one of the brightest stars of the Harlem Renaissance, but he also met some lifelong friends, including Countee Cullen, who was a student at New York University when Langston came to the city, and Zora Neale Hurston, who already had her own fame, as she had been writing earlier than Langston. Even though she was eleven years older than Langston, they remained friends for life.

When the Renaissance hit its stride, many new innovations came to Harlem. Duke Ellington was important to the movement with his jazz music. Others were innovative with dance presentations, art, and all kinds of literature. People flocked to the Cotton Club, the Savoy Ballroom, and the continuous shows that were booked at the Apollo Theater. These new innovations of the era gave new interpretations to African American culture.

After being immersed in the Harlem Renaissance for a number of years, Langston decided he wanted to see the world. He was getting a few royalties from some of his published poems, but in order to make more money, he got himself hired on freighters that were going to many faraway places. His travels took him to Europe, Africa, and Asia, including Russia. He was even brought before the McCarthy Senate hearings to testify as to whether he was a Communist or not.

Even though Langston did not return to Columbia University, he eventually got a college degree in 1929 from Lincoln University in Pennsylvania. As fate would have it, he met Thurgood Marshall at Lincoln. Thurgood graduated from Lincoln in 1928. After his graduation from college, Langston traveled to Haiti, Cuba, and the USSR between the years of 1930 and 1932.

Langston Hughes did so many things during his busy and colorful life that in the interest of space and time, I will give a summary of how well he did over the years. Before his life was over, he had written at least fifty books. He wrote an uncountable number of poems; many were published. His friendship with Vachel Lindsay accounted for him getting much of his work published. It is also important to note that he became a regular columnist for the black weekly newspaper, the

Chicago Defender. The *Chicago Defender* had been his favorite newspaper as a child, because that was where he could keep up with what was happening in the areas of black America. He was awarded the highly acclaimed Springarn Medal from the NAACP in 1960. He did some writing for the *Crisis*, the magazine of the NAACP. He also personally knew W. E. B. Dubois, who helped found the NAACP.

For his books entitled *First Book of Africa* and *African Treasury*, he received the NIAL Award in 1961. He also wrote five books in 1961, including *Black Nativity*, which received high acclaim.

In 1967, Langston had to be taken to New York City Hospital for an emergency operation. He survived the operation but got a serious infection and passed away a few hours later. The date of Langston Hughes's death was May 20, 1967. No one could argue that Langston was not the heart and soul of the Harlem Renaissance. He was our most prolific writer. He was always on the move, and for that reason, he never married or had any children. Langston Hughes's ashes are buried at the site of the Schomburg Center for Research in Black Culture. The Schomburg is a part of the New York City library system and is located at the corner of Lenox Avenue and 135th Street.

Your net worth to the world is usually determined by what remains after your bad habits are subtracted from your good ones.

—Benjamin Franklin

CHAPTER 10

In 2013, Has Martin Luther King Jr.'s Dream Been Realized or Not?

Fifty years ago this past August, Dr. King made his never-to-be-forgotten "I Have a Dream" speech. More black people than ever before trekked to Washington, DC, for the march on Washington to show solidarity in the desire to bring about positive change in the conditions that African Americans were still facing at the time. Jim Crow was supposed to have fallen two years later, when the Civil Rights Act was passed. However, black individuals still had a long way to go in becoming accepted as first-class citizens of America.

Standing on the National Mall with the Lincoln Memorial as his backdrop, Dr. King made a speech that will never be forgotten. It is heralded as one of the greatest speeches ever made by any American citizen. His speech is motivation that we can always look back on when we require some kind of inspiration to lift us up. Before he concluded the speech, Dr. King said something that we should never forget. The central, major part of his speech was a challenge to us and to the people who did not care for us. The most important sentence was "One day little white boys and girls, and little black boys and girls will be able to play together because they will be judged by the content of their character rather than by the color of their skin."

When Dr. King uttered those words, I am sure he felt that those words would be memorable for us as a guide. They would be the template, the fire, and the energy that we, as a race, would always be able to reach back for in order to gain strength to move forward. It was the speech that would help us as we went forward in our attempts to climb that important "mountain of character" that he revealed to us on that August day in 1963. Those words will always be emblazoned in our minds, and we should always remember that character is one of the most important qualities we need if our race is going to rise in the eyes of other ethnicities, especially in the eyes of American Caucasians. Dr. King knew that character was that most-important ingredient that could at least slow racists down, if not stop them from uttering despicable things about us as a people. The reasons were obvious. We could show them that we were better than the people they had defined us as in the past. We would show them, as the future unfolded, that we had as much dignity and pride as everyone else. We would show all of the other ethnicities that we were a group of people to be admired, even liked, because our not-seen-before behaviors and actions were on par with every other race. People would start to see us in a new light. That light would render our previous haters to a state of color blindness, just as Dr. King had predicted. Our brownness or blackness would have absolutely nothing to do with how much we were accepted or not accepted as decent human beings.

Dr. King was, all through the early civil rights years, a man who had massive struggles with being insulted, treated rudely, threatened, and quickly thrown in jail for civil disobedience. Dr. King was on a serious mission. That mission was to get us the respect and equality we deserved as black people. From the time he accepted his silent oath to make things better for us until the time he lost his life by assassination in Memphis, Tennessee, in 1968, he was relentless in trying to lift up the black people of America.

It is now time to step back and put things in perspective. First, we need to have a serious discussion regarding what character means to us and what it meant for Dr. King. To get into this matter, I have consulted *Webster's New World Dictionary.*

I found a total of fourteen different definitions for *character.* However, we need to concentrate on only seven of the definitions, numbers five through eleven. Those are as follows:

1. A distinctive trust, quality, or attribute

2. An essential quality, nature, kind or sort

3. The pattern of behavior or personality found in an individual or a group; moral constitution

4. Moral strength, self-discipline, fortitude

5. Reputation, especially good reputation

6. A statement about the behavior or qualities of a person; Ex: As a character reference

7. Status or position

When we seriously read through each of the above definitions, we can unmistakably understand what Dr. King had in mind when he spoke of "the content of our character" that he foresaw for us as we, as a race, bravely marched on into the future. So take the time to look once more at the above list, and I am sure you will find that each definition has to do with positives or positivity. Dr. King realized that these were (and they still are) the kinds of things that would and could lift our feet out of any quagmire or onerous, burdensome, or oppressive situations that might confront us. In his "Dream" speech, he attempted to give us a key as to how we could all eventually be able to walk tall and with well-earned pride in ourselves as individuals and also in our race as a whole. Most of all, he offered himself as a role model that all of us would be able to copy. He gave us the ideal of what a real leader is supposed to be.

Let's refer back to the question offered as the title of this chapter, now that we have looked back to the 1963 dream of Dr. King: After fifty years, has his dream been realized or not? Sadly, after the passing of fifty years, the answer to the question is a resounding no.

Why? Please allow me to count the ways and reasons.

1. Do we honestly feel that Dr. King would feel good about the strides we have made over the past fifty years when it comes to educational gains? Do we feel he would hold his head up and be able to brag about how much further we have come with all of the educational aid now available to us with the wink of an eye or a snap of our fingers? Let us not forget that *computer* was like a foreign word fifty years ago. Now we cannot even say we don't have a computer because we are too poor. Computers are available to all of us at almost any library. Furthermore, libraries are full of books readily available to us.

2. Do we feel that Dr. King would believe that most of our black parents of today are doing the things necessary, including investments in time, to raise successful black children for the future?

3. Do we believe Dr. King would feel pride if he knew that in 2013, there was a 72 percent out-of-wedlock birth rate for African American children? That means that seven out of ten black homes with children are likely to have no significant male present on a daily basis. This statistic is particularly important at this time, when we are seeing many young black males falling by the wayside in one way or another.

4. Would Dr. King be proud of the manner in which our unmarried black fathers abandon their offspring, both socially and financially? Here we must remember that other ethnicities look upon the male as the protector and the provider for his children and their mother. This arrangement is even true in the animal kingdom.

5. How could Dr. King be proud of the fact that such a large number of our black children are failing to complete high school? This is especially disheartening when we separate out our young black boys. What can we give as a reasonable or acceptable excuse, since public school is free? The only excuse is not a good excuse, and that excuse is a lack of interest.

6. Do we feel Dr. King would be willing to go out protesting or complaining about the high unemployment rate for blacks? The unemployment rate is higher for young black males than for the high rate of our people at large. Dr. King would be aware that most of these young men are not dedicated to doing what needs to be done to prepare themselves for even average work competency. They feel that learning the necessary skills is too hard. Their answer is that they can take the easy way out, which is to quit school and hit the streets.

7. Does anyone reading this feel that a man like Dr. King, who comported himself with such pride and dignity, would be anything less than disgusted when every other young black male (and some not so young) is walking around in public with his pants hanging off his behind and his underwear showing to the public? Again, what ever happened to shame or stigma?

8. Similarly, do we feel Dr. King would wonder what happened to us when he witnessed young women, and

some young men, getting up out of bed and walking to the store in their pajama bottoms? Such actions imply a lack of hygienic care.

9. There can be no doubt that Dr. King would be spinning in his grave if there was some way for him to know how many young black men—some just fifteen, sixteen, and seventeen years old—are going around killing other black people. New initiates to black street gangs are out in force now, and it makes no difference to them whether they shoot some member of a rival gang, a young preschool child, or some older person. But the common denominator seems to be that they always manage to shoot another black person. That means that we are now our own enemies, often shooting ourselves. Worst of all was a young boy who was shot in his stroller when the shooter shot at the father and missed.

10. Younger blacks under forty-five years old might not understand this next query. However, I am sure those of us who saw Dr. King when he was alive and saw how hard he worked to help raise us to a point of equality will readily understand the next statement. If Dr. King could hear any of the filth, profanity, and other disrespectful vulgarities that the mouths of gangster rappers spew, he would be hurt and angry. I cannot believe he would not care how despicable they are in the ways they can influence young children. I also know that he would not be pleased with a group of people who have no problem going to prison. In fact, they feel serving time in prison is helpful to them, as it gives them "street cred." That in itself says that these are people who live by a thug, hoodlum, and criminal philosophy. These kinds of individuals are far from what Dr. King had in mind for us when he left this earth. I'm sure Dr. King would not be able to comprehend that fellow so-called musicians go

into nightclubs with their posses and provoke each other to the point where they hurl $2,000 bottles of champagne at each other. That kind of behavior is what our haters from other ethnicities love to see. And when they see that kind of atrocious behavior, they have no problem saying, "See how *they* act?"

11. Lastly, there is no way Dr. King would understand why so many of us were in prison at the end of 2013. By the latest Google figures, black non-Hispanic males were in prison at a rate of 4,347 per 100,000. Whites were in prison at a rate of 678 per 100,000. And Hispanics were in prison at a rate of 1,775 per 100,000. So who is going to jail more than anyone else? Black males. The above figures are just through 2010. With all of the young black killers who have been already apprehended but are sitting in jail awaiting trial for all of the rampant killings and black-on-black shootings around the nation, the figure will more than likely rise. No matter how you look at the imprisonment of young black males, we have to admit that these people are not being thrown in jail for years just for civil disobedience. These people made a decision to become criminals, and they got caught. When I was growing up in the old Jim Crow South in Georgia, I had a teenage cousin who shoplifted from Woolworth's five-and-dime store. He was tried and sent to the reformatory for juveniles for over nine years. In other words, he went in as a teenager and came out as a fully grown man. He was the son of my father's sister. My father took me to see my cousin on two occasions, and that was enough for me to decide that I would never make that fateful decision to commit a crime.

I now want to spend some time on the other key word in Dr. King's speech on character: *content*. Going to *Webster's New World Dictionary* again, I found two definitions that apply to or fit with character. Meaning one deals with happiness and satisfaction, as in general contentment. But the content that Dr. King was referring to was content having to do with volume— for example, the content in a medicine or a table of contents. A high content, when connected to character, is good. A low content is not good. A simpler way to explain good content of character is to look back at the eleven examples Dr. King would not endorse on the list of shame I gave earlier. If we took any example on the list and reversed it, that would rate as building up the content of our character. Let's take, for example, the sagging-pants trend among our young black men. If that were reversed, we could say that our young men are people we can be proud of, because as a group, they always seem to look appropriate and presentable when in public. That would count as showing an improvement in the content of our character.

Back in 1990, a young professor of English at San Jose State University in California, Shelby Steele, wrote a book titled *The Content of Our Character*. His motivation was, of course, the Martin L. King Jr. "I Have a Dream" speech of 1963.

Mr. Steele's thesis was that he felt we were continuing to do ourselves no good as a race, because we were still too oriented in being victims. Let us not forget that this was twenty-seven years after the 1963 speech. Professor Steele, a black man himself, said,

> It was the emphasis on mass action in the sixties that made the victim-focused black identity a necessity. But in the nineties and beyond, when racial advancement will come only through a multitude of individual advancements, this form of identity inadvertently adds itself to the forces that hold us back. Hard work, education, individual initiative, stable family life, property ownership—these have always been the means by which ethnic groups have moved ahead in America.

At this point, our race seems to be undergoing a kind of domino effect. Each sorry act of neglect, negligence, disinterest, or immorality moves us on to some other area of lowness on the character scale. Let us look at those born in 1980. They were born twenty-seven years after the "I Have a Dream" speech. They were born twelve years after Dr. King's assassination. As a consequence of them having parents who never invested enough time, or any time, in letting them know how much Dr. King did in the way of moving us forward, they know little more than that there is a Martin L. King Drive, Boulevard, Street, or Avenue in almost every city. Many have so little interest in the hard fight that Dr. King waged that they do not even care to go vote on polling dates. It seems too many of us continue to move from one act of disinterest and lack of appreciation to another. Each time we make these backward moves, we continuously lower the content of our character as a people.

For many years, we heard the same statement over and over when it came to the poor behavior of our young black men. That statement was "These black boys and young men do not have any role models." Lo and behold, in 2008, a black man by the name of Barack Obama ran for president of the United States, and he won. So now young black boys have the greatest role model they could have ever hoped for. But if a poll were taken, the results would probably be embarrassing for us, because I think the number of people who ever took time to listen to an Obama speech would be low. The reasoning I am using is how their actions and behavior have slipped backward.

I want to make just a few more comments on where we are in terms of realizing the dream of Dr. King. In the magazine the *Week*, in the September 6, 2013, issue, President Obama said, "We would dishonor those heroes who marched on the capital 50 years ago to demand equal rights for black Americans. If we somehow suggest the work of this nation is somehow complete." His major point was that economic inequality is the nation's "great unfinished business."

Representative John Lewis of Georgia said we have made much progress since he took part in the original march. In his speech commemorating the 50th Anniversary of the March on Washington (8/24/2013), however, he also said "We have another fight. There are forces, there are people who want to take us back."

The *Philadelphia Inquirer* noted that Barack Obama's election as president offers "striking evidence of progress. But let's not fool ourselves: This is no post-racial society." In every aspect of life, a clear racial divide remains: the black unemployment rate stands at 12.6 percent, nearly twice that of whites, while African Americans are incarcerated at nearly six times the rate of whites.

The *National Review* wrote,

> Don't blame racism for the black community's continued struggles. Blame the decrepitude of today's civil rights movement. With racial discrimination all but vanquished, King's supposed heirs, like Al Sharpton, would rather race-bait over issues like voter ID Laws and the Trayvon Martin shooting than confront the real, deep-seated problems afflicting the black community—drugs, lousy schools, and the collapse of marriage.

B.D. Colen of the *Atlantic* wrote,

> There is no doubt that much has changed. That includes the election of a black president - unimaginable in 1963 But our prisons are bursting at the seams with black men, most of our urban school systems are failing dismally, and it is not yet safe for a black teenager wearing a hoodie to walk through a white neighborhood.

Mike Gonzales wrote in the *New York Post,*

> If anything is holding back progress in this country it is well-meaning government attempts to rescue people from poverty. Such programs create perverse incentives, discouraging people from taking jobs or getting married. The out-of-wedlock birthrate among blacks is now 72 percent. That's the real obstacle to equality.

Charles M. Blow, who is black, wrote in the *New York Times,*

> Ultimately, we are still living in two separate Americas. Polls show that most black people still feel they are treated less fairly by the police, by the courts, at work, and in schools. Yet few whites agree, expressing weariness—if not downright hostility over continued discussion of the role of race in America. I wish I could be more optimistic, but it all leaves an uneasy gnawing in my gut.

As we come to the end of this chapter, you have my thoughts, and you have some expressions of others. I think we will all agree that we still have a lot of work to do to reach Dr. King's dream.

———*ᴐᴠᴠ*———

There will be no separate inspirational person for this chapter, because the person whom the chapter was devoted to is the inspirational person: Dr. Martin Luther King Jr.

Dr. Martin Luther King, Jr.

Dr. King was born in Atlanta, Georgia on January 15, 1929. Most people are not aware that he was named Michael King, Jr. at birth. That was because his father's birth name was Michael King.

Reverend Michael King, Sr. would become the pastor of the Ebenezer Baptist Church in Atlanta. As Rev. King, Sr. pursued his spiritual readings, he became so impressed with the works and the history of the German theologian, Martin Luther, that he changed his name to Martin Luther. The son, Michael King, Jr. decided to follow suit and change his name to remain a true, same-name son as his father.

Dr. King was the middle child of Michael and Roberta Williams. He attended Washington High School in Atlanta. That was in the days when Washington High was the major high school for blacks in Atlanta.

Martin, Jr. was a very smart and precocious child. He went on to enroll at Morehouse College in Atlanta, Ga. At the age of fifteen. He graduated from Morehouse in 1948. He went on to Crozer Theological Seminary in Chester, Pennsylvania, earning a Bachelor of Divinity degree in 1951 and a Ph. D. from Boston University in 1955.

The now young Dr. Rev. Martin Luther King, Jr. was chosen to become the pastor of the Dexter Avenue Baptist Church in Montgomery, Alabama. It needs to be stated here that Dr. King met Coretta Scott while in Boston. He would marry Ms. Scott, and from their union four children were born. The children were Yolanda, Martin III, Dexter, and Bernice.

In hindsight, it seems as if Dr. King's appointment to a church in Montgomery, Alabama may have been kind of a predestination. It seems this way because he was in Montgomery when Rosa Parks was arrested for refusing to move to the back of a Montgomery city bus. The Rosa Parks incident occurred in December of 1955. Many are unaware that there was a fifteen year old girl who was arrested for the same reason, but prior to the arrest of Rosa Parks. This girl's name was Claudette Colvin. Dr. King along with the NAACP thought they had a good case to move on with the Colvin arrest. But one thing deterred them from moving ahead with this young girl's incident. They discovered that the girl was pregnant, and they knew at that point this girl's future would be damaged, possibly completely destroyed, if the fact of her pregnancy went public (Taylor Branch. *Parting The Waters - American in the King Years 1954-63.* 1988. Pg. 123).

In December of 1955 when forty-two year old Rosa Parks refused to move to the back of the bus, in violation of a city ordinance, the NAACP and Dr. King knew they had a case they could move on. The same night of Ms. Park's arrest would find Dr. King along with the NAACP leadership and other black local leaders spelling out their plans for a bus boycott. There is no need to go any further to declare that this was the beginning of Dr. King's meteoric rise to become, arguably, the most famous and legendary person to work for black equality.

In 1957 Dr. King, along with sixty ministers and black activists started the SCLC (Southern Christian Leadership Conference). The arrests for civil disobedience are a well-known part of the Civil Rights Movement's history. Dr. King's letter from the Birmingham jail will never be forgotten. We have already covered the August, 1963 "I Have A Dream" speech in Washington, D.C. Dr. King would also receive the Nobel Peace Prize in 1964, at the age of thirty-five.

This man never looked back in his efforts to do whatever he could for black people once he got rolling in 1955. It is so amazing that he would accomplish so much in thirteen years. He was on the job for us, trying to help the black sanitation workers of Memphis, Tennessee receive fair pay for their labor, when his life was taken in April of 1968.

It is recommended that the readers of this book find Dr. King's speech, "Where Do We Go From Here." The speech can be found in its entirety via the internet, so the reader can simply use Google to find it. It is probably the next most famous of his speeches, after the "I Have A Dream" speech and the "I've Been to the Mountaintop" speech. Dr. King's "Where Do We Go From Here" speech was delivered in 1967 at the 11th Annual SCLC Convention in Atlanta, Georgia.

The only place where success comes before work is in the dictionary.

—Vidal Sassoon

CHAPTER 11

Some Last Words

We have now arrived at the point in this long discussion, or open letter, where I see a need for some reiteration and also some expansion.

One of the major points I wanted to convey, if not the most important point, was to make a special case for the people of our race to become more serious about obtaining an adequate education. My first two chapters mainly focused on education.

We cannot start too early in taking on the challenge of developing our children's interest in doing the necessary work to, at minimum, complete high school. The second chapter noted what compulsory education affords one. Children need to learn early on not to expect what high school graduates will have available if they opt to drop out in the ninth or tenth grade.

Furthermore, society at large does not give much respect to high school dropouts, particularly because they are looked upon as being not too bright. Another reason is that people cannot understand why a child would turn down the greatest gift of all time—the free gift of education, there for the taking.

Those who refuse to take the opportunity to receive this gift of learning should know, in no uncertain terms, that they can expect to be called dumb, ignorant, and unintelligent. In reality, they are all three, and they have only themselves to blame. Taking the time to become educated insulates one from derogatory labels. If you're educated, people call you smart, bright, and intelligent. In fact, spending that extra time to become a learned person can turn one's life around.

Some Buds of Promise

There are a few people I feel deserve some special mention because they are young but already understand what I am saying.

Because these young people have been able to understand so early in life what I am continuously preaching as my favorite sermons, they demonstrate that they are able to understand the ingredients for building character and foundations for future success. The two youngsters I will write about are aware of what they will need to garner respect for themselves, and they also know they will always have the ability to be proud of themselves.

1. A-Sean (Pronounced "A-Shun") Johnson

A-Sean is a young black boy who began to get a lot of notice in the city of Chicago when he was just eight years old. Why all of this notice? A-Sean was attending Marcus Garvey Elementary School, which was on a list of schools to be closed. A-Sean let himself be heard. By the time this young boy was nine years old, he was drawing massive crowds wherever he spoke. The speaking voice of this youngster was no measly, awkward voice. He drew so many to hear him because he spoke with the poise and timbre of a seasoned orator.

A-Sean was still getting more attention as he reached the age of ten. It was then that he went to the Martin L. King Jr. Fiftieth Anniversary of the 1963 march on Washington. At the event in 2013, A-Sean became the youngest speaker ever. In 1963, that honor had gone to Representative John Lewis. This young boy, at the tender age of ten, had already etched his name in history as a fighter for black causes and black progress.

When A-Sean spoke in Washington in 2013, he picked up more admirers. More importantly, he won over Mayor Rahm Emanuel of Chicago, and the decision to leave Marcus Garvey Elementary School open was made after A-Sean went on his speaking tours.

After A-Sean's attendance at the 2013 Washington, DC, MLK commemoration, he was invited as a guest to the White House, where he had a face-to-face audience with President Obama. The major point is that we do have some young black children in this country who can help us shed the negative labels. We are at a point where we can use all of the A-Seans we can find.

2. Malala Yousafzai

Malala Yousafzai is a young girl who is not black, but she can say a lot of valuable things to black children. She has much of the same kind of wisdom that A-Sean has. That is the kind of inspiration from which one can draw interest in things that matter. Malala is a native of Pakistan. I first learned about her when I was reading the *New York Daily News*' editorial page on October 15, 2013. On Thursday, October 14, 2013, Malala was awarded the European Parliament's Sakharov Prize for Freedom of Thought. This young person had just recently reached the age of sixteen. Because of what she had done, and also what was done to her, she was on a short list as a possible winner of the Nobel Peace Prize. She did not win in 2013, but she might be mentioned again in 2014.

Malala catapulted to international fame when she was living at home in Pakistan's Swat Valley. She was also attending school. One day, a Taliban would-be assassin shot her in the neck and head as she was going home on the school bus. The reason for this attack was because the Taliban forbids females from attending school. One bullet passed through her head and became lodged near her spinal cord. Miraculously, Malala survived. One would think that after such a close shave with death, she would give up and not ever have any plans of attending school again. But this brave, determined young girl was just beginning to fight. She started to speak out more loudly and clearly than before on the rights of everyone to go to school. Her own words were that all boys and girls should be able to attend school and get an education. Her reason was that everyone should be treated equally. She even went on to say she hoped that at some time, the daughters of the Taliban, or any other terrorist group, would have the opportunity to go to school.

I felt that I had to mention Malala's story, as it should provide great motivation for black girls and boys here in the USA. If our young people would take the time to study our own history, they would understand that there was a time when black individuals were not allowed to learn how to read or write and also not able to go to school. But too many of our children—not all, but too many—lack appreciation for what so many of our forefathers went through to help us reach a higher level of living.

It is a pity that we have, at this time, decided to take the low road rather than that high road, especially after many gave their lives to lift us up to success, decency, and dignity. Over the months that I let my mind roam, I decided that I wanted this book to be a semi–history lesson. To do so, I introduced inspirational black people at the end of every chapter.

At any rate, but for the grace of God, we would not have heard of Malala. And that means she would not have been thought of as a potential Nobel Prize winner. The upside is that A-Sean and Malala have had a tremendous impact. But the downside is this: How many of our young black children have not heard of either of them? If I wanted to go out and make some quick money, I could make a bet about the results of asking twenty young black girls or boys, "Have you ever heard of A-Sean Johnson or Malala Yousafzai?" You know what they would say? They would say, "Who?" Maybe one or two would know whom I was talking about. The reason is that we do not care to know things. Or maybe I should say that we are not interested in things that have a major impact on our lives. I hate to have to say this, but when those Tea Party people say, "We need to take our country back," too many of us are helping them take it back. How far back? All the way back to when we were helpless.

I was a black child of the 1940s and 1950s. Those were big-time Jim Crow years. They were the years when African Americans could not go into some front doors of establishments. They could not dare to want to eat in most restaurants. It was a time when there were "colored" and "white" water fountains, and the same for toilets at gas stations. I always went to schools considered inadequate. I went to an elementary school that had five black female teachers who taught eight grades. Therefore, one teacher taught first grade and what was known as "primer grade" in the same classroom. Half of the students sat on one side of the room, and half sat on the other side. One teacher taught both the second and third grades. Lastly, the principal taught the six and seventh grades the same way. The school was a small wooden clapboard structure. We got our books secondhand when the whites got new books. But guess what? We still read the same things the whites read before they shipped their books over to us. Those of us who had interest in learning were able to learn. At no time from the primer grade through the twelfth grade did we ever have one breakfast or lunch provided for us at school. However, again, we who were interested in getting an education learned. I say this to make the point that you would have a hard time attempting to sell me on the idea that schools today are lousy.

—⁓—

There are a few other short stories of hope I feel I need to mention before the end of this book.

The Steve and Marjorie Harvey Foundation

Steve Harvey, the comedian, actor, radio personality, and game-show host, and his wife take part in mentoring black young boys and men. Note that of all the labels mentioned above for Steve, none of them was "black leader." But his mentoring program is making him out to be more of a black leader than those who feel they have that title all to themselves.

The Harveys began their campaign in October 2012. They were hoping to reach one hundred thousand black boys by the end of 2013. The information on whether or not they reached their goal is not available as I am writing this, at the end of January 2014.

They have started groups in eleven cities. The order and beginning dates are as follows:

Los Angeles – October 2012

Chicago – November 2012

Washington, DC – January 2013

Columbia, SC – February 2013

New York and New Jersey – March 2013

Philadelphia – April 2013

Dallas – June 2013

Los Angeles, location number two – June 2013

Newark – July 2013

Las Vegas – August 2013

Detroit – September 2013

This mentoring campaign has a mission of promoting black male achievement. The Harveys also want to create strong male relationships for black boys who lack such relationships. A major goal is to succeed in shifting the image and perception of black men and boys inside and outside of African American communities.

The Jim Brown I-Can All-Star Basketball Program

Jim Brown is a man known for his great feats as a running back for the Cleveland Browns. He is a longtime NFL Hall of Famer. People do not know him primarily as a black leader, but that is a title he is earning as his program continues to gain recognition in Los Angeles. He won over one of the best-known former Cripps and got him to run the program. The former gangbanger and former pro basketball player's name is Rudolph "Rockhead" Johnson. The program has its center in the Watts section of Los Angeles. Four gangs claim that area as part of their turf. But oddly, though graffiti covers most of the buildings in the area, there is none on the program's basketball center. The names of these gangs are the East Coast Cripps, the Kitchen Cripps, the Grape Street Cripps, and Florencia.

Rockhead Johnson, who is now forty-eight years old, was one of the most feared and meanest Cripps before Jim Brown turned him around. Because of his reputation, he can manage such a program in an area that continues to be plagued with crime and violence. Rockhead does not stand for any fights at the center. He has been shot at and stabbed, and he spent a third of his life incarcerated. Johnson's own words are a hymn to Jim Brown's grace. He said, "Jim Brown finally helped me to see senselessness in us killing each other over red and blue rags."

Colonel Gregory E. Collins and the Harlem Youth Marines

Colonel Gregory E. Collins started the Harlem Youth Marines in the Harlem community of New York as a not-for-profit organization over thirty-three years ago, in 1980. During the time that this organization has been going, it has gotten more than two thousand boys from the Harlem streets to participate in the program. The boys are from seven to twenty years old. Under the direction of Colonel Collins, the Harlem Youth Marines meet weekly from 5:00 p.m. until 8:00 p.m. at the 369th Harlem State Armory, which is located at 2366 Fifth Avenue.

The mission is to prevent drug abuse, reduce the rate of high school dropouts, and combat the influence of gangs on young men and women by providing positive, motivating messages with the use of youth and adult forces. The organization uses military discipline to foster confidence.

A further mission is to help these involved youths achieve goals they can use to improve themselves and their communities. The organization's staff also stresses good grooming, drills, ceremonies, customs, courtesy, uniformity in rank structure, chain of command, and physical training. They review school report cards and offer tutoring to cadets who need help with schoolwork. They even make home visits when necessary. There are also fun activities, such as sports, camping, hiking, parades, and ceremonies that are part of community events.

I see this organization as one that is highly useful if boys in Harlem would take part. I also see Colonel Gregory E. Collins as an unsung hero for doing such positive work over thirty-three years.

Black Girls Rock

I do not feel that many black people would try to make the argument that young black girls or women are as much to blame for our negative stigmas as the young black males. However, our young women also need some guidance to help them think straight.

Ms. Beverly Bond founded Black Girls Rock in 2006. Her vision was to start an organization with the primary goal of mentoring and teaching young black girls and women how they can become empowered. This organization has grown to a point where it has an annual major television awards show. The show aims to celebrate the accomplishments of exceptional women of color. The women whom the organization selects have all made outstanding contributions in their careers and serve as inspiration for the young girls, providing examples of what they can hope to achieve and how they can be positive role models in their own communities. Ms. Bond herself received the Image Award from the NAACP in the category "Outstanding Variety Series or Special."

Ms. Bond also formed a bond with BET, did prior mentoring, and worked as a philanthropist and community leader. All of the above qualifies her to be the executive director of an organization like Black Girls Rock. It is also important to point out that Ms. Bond has been on *Ebony* magazine's Power 100 List from 2008 to 2012—five consecutive years. This top honor, along with the others she has received, makes her a major role model for the young girls and women she works with.

To end this piece on Black Girls Rock, it is worthwhile to mention that their top award for 2013 went to Mrs. Marian Wright Edelman. Mrs. Edelman is now seventy-four years old and is a black woman for other black women to emulate. She is a well-known civil rights activist, the founder of the Children's Defense Fund, and a lawyer for the NAACP.

Mrs. Edelman went to Spelman College in Atlanta and then on to Yale Law School prior to becoming a lawyer for the NAACP. She is also a prolific writer, especially on the issues of racial inequality in the USA.

―ᔕᔕ―

Very Last Words

Black parents, please seriously consider taking your children to church early in their lives. This is something I beg you to do, whether you are two parents or a single mother. It is important that your child or children have a strong foundation early on, learning the meaning of morals and the difference between right and wrong. "Train up a child in the way he should go, and when he is old he will not depart from it" (Proverbs 22:6).

www.ingramcontent.com/pod-product-compliance
Lightning Source LLC
Chambersburg PA
CBHW020535290526
45786CB00002B/883